The Literary Criticism of

MATTHEW ARNOLD

T0340660

"Yet he is in some respects the most satisfactory
man of letters of his age."

T.S. Eliot, *The Use of Poetry and the Use of Criticism*

The Literary Criticism of
MATTHEW ARNOLD

LETTERS TO CLOUGH, THE 1853 PREFACE,
AND SOME ESSAYS

FLEMMING OLSEN

sussex
ACADEMIC
PRESS
Brighton • Chicago • Toronto

2 4 6 8 10 9 7 5 3 1

First published 2015, in Great Britain by
SUSSEX ACADEMIC PRESS
PO Box 139
Eastbourne BN24 9BP

SUSSEX ACADEMIC PRESS
Independent Publishers Group
814 N. Franklin Street, Chicago, IL 60610

and in Canada by
SUSSEX ACADEMIC PRESS (CANADA)
24 Ranee Avenue, Toronto, Ontario, M6A 1M6

British Library Cataloguing in Publication Data
A CIP catalogue record for this book is available from the British Library.

Library of Congress Cataloguing-in-Publication Data
Applied for.

ISBN 978-1-84519-710-0 (paperback)

Typeset & designed by Sussex Academic Press, Brighton & Eastbourne.
Printed TJ International, Padstow, Cornwall.

CONTENTS

PREFACE

Many of the ideas that appear in Arnold's *Preface* of 1853 and in his later essays are suggested in the letters that Arnold wrote to his friend Arthur Hugh Clough. The interest of the *Preface* resides in the fact that it is a young poet's attempt to establish some criteria for what poetry ought to be if it was to live up to his idiosyncratic ideals.

Arnold found the Romantic idiom outworn. The Romantic poets, he found, "did not know enough", their theoretical foundation was weak, and they were mainly preoccupied by creating effects of harmony and imagery, whereas Arnold's main concern was what literature could be used for, could do.

The Neo-Classicists had their system of rules and their models to imitate, especially Homer and Horace. No such code existed in the mid-nineteenth century, and Arnold did not wish to revive it. Yet it is interesting to see how closely related the precepts of the *Preface* are to the rules laid down in antiquity for classical tragedy – the only "kind" for which a fairly detailed set of principles existed.

Literary criticism never became Arnold's prime concern. As the analysis of some of the essays will show, literature was, in Arnold's perception, meant to communicate a message rather than impress by its structure or by formal sophistication. He did acknowledge what he called *architectonicè*, wholeness or a synthesis, but he was only superficially interested in the parts that went into such wholes. The modern theories of coalescence between content and form were outside the contemporary paradigm. However, the fact that literary criticism was to Arnold an ancillary discipline is not tantamount to saying that it is devoid of interest.

In 2012, Sussex Academic Press published my book *Eliot's Objective Correlative. Tradition or Individual Talent*. In the process of collecting material for the book, I was struck by Eliot's ambivalent attitude to Arnold – now reluctantly admiring, now decidedly patronizing. Eliot never seemed able to liberate himself from the influence of Arnold. What in Arnold's critical oeuvre attracted and at the same time repelled Eliot? That question led me to an in-depth analysis of Arnold as a literary critic.

This book begins with an examination of Arnold's letters to Clough, where "it all started" and proceeds with a close reading of the 1853 *Preface*. A look at some of the later literary essays rounds off the picture of Arnold as a literary critic.

The Literary Criticism of
MATTHEW
ARNOLD

Introduction

Wordsworth

Wordsworth's *Preface to the Second Edition of Lyrical Ballads* (1800) advanced an idiosyncratic and, as demonstrated by Coleridge, untenable theory about the language of poetry, where Wordsworth made himself the spokesman of a change of paradigm after the "poetic diction" prevalent in much 18th century poetry. It is true that the distinction between imagination and fancy, later to be elaborated by Coleridge, was first propounded here, but the preface covers only a narrow aspect of the literary spectrum. Compared with Arnold's *Preface*, the interesting thing is that Wordsworth refers to his own poetry and uses it as the centre from which his theory radiates.

Coleridge

In *Biographia Literaria* (1817), Coleridge gives an account of his philosophical development and his present position. It is a complicated and very personal document, and only very remotely a piece of literary criticism. Coleridge's purpose is to distance himself from association psychology, and the distinction between imagination and fancy, which he took over from Wordsworth, has made the *Biographia* a landmark of English criticism. However, the book lies within the realm of philosophical speculation rather than literary criticism. Thus, the theory is not properly illustrated with examples from literature.

Coleridge's essay from 1803, Concerning *Poetry and the Pleasure to be derived from it*, contains a good many platitudes and seems to be a routine work from the hands of a writer whose allegiance lay elsewhere. It was given a fairly cold reception.

Shelley

Shelley wrote *A Defence of Poetry* because he felt it incumbent on him to defend poets and poetry against attacks levelled against them, down through the centuries, for immorality. Though written in 1822, the book was not published until 1840, i.e. posthumously. The book is heavily indebted to Plato's idea of poetic inspiration, and Shelley was convinced of the restorative powers of literature. The *Defence* is an array of positively loaded superlatives, but the reader looks in vain for any argumentation. *A Defence of* Poetry lives up to its title and can be considered a work of literary criticism only in a very restricted sense of the word.

Leigh Hunt

Judging from the title of his essay *What Is Poetry?* Leigh Hunt seemed to face the issue squarely. The essay was printed in a book called *Imagination and Fancy*, which was published in 1840. It should be added, though, that Hunt never really grasped the implications of Coleridge's famous pair.[1]

What Is Poetry? is not and was not intended to be an *ars poetica* in the Horatian sense.[2] On the other hand, it cannot be brushed aside as merely a collection of purple patches, not least because it is suffused with Hunt's genuine enthusiasm for his subject.

It is characteristic of the four authors that, unlike the Neo-Classicists, they were not interested in compartmentalization, hierarchies and rules. And they did not refer to classical precedent to gain support for their views. Such axioms as they leant on were extrapolations of their own experiences and idiosyncrasies.

CHAPTER ONE

THE INTELLECTUAL LANDSCAPE OF THE MID-VICTORIAN AGE

The first occurrence of the word 'literature' in the sense of 'literary productions as a whole, the writings of a country or a period, or of the word in general' is recorded by the *OED* in 1812, so, by the time Arnold wrote his *Preface*, the term literature in its modern helicopter meaning was a fairly recent acquisition. However, as yet literature *per se* was not an object of study, so Arnold's *Preface* did not inscribe itself in a tradition of literary theorizing. No critical schools existed, literary movements were not properly investigated, themes were not pursued, and genres and their requirements were largely ignored.

Thus, a modern reader is struck by the lack of terminological precision in contemporary prefaces and essays, chiefly because poets talk about 'poetry' where we would say 'literature' or 'poetry' or 'a literary work'. In Shelley's *Defence of Poetry*, 'poetry' is obviously intended to refer to literature in general. Leigh Hunt exemplifies 'poetry' with a lavish collection of examples from drama, and Arnold's *Preface* is, to a great extent, tailored to the pattern of Aristotle's *Poetics*. None of those writers ever use the word 'literature'.

By 'literary criticism', the contemporary intellectual opinion makers understood the evaluation of the content of a written text. Mid-Victorian critics were not primarily concerned with literature as a union of content and form, or as an aesthetic object: Stuart Mill was a social philosopher, Ruskin and Pater were aesthetes, and Arnold's main interest was in social and religious issues rather than in linguistic technicalities. It is true that Hippolyte Taine, the French critic, in 1864 established some criteria for the creation of a literary work (*la race, le milieu, le moment*). However, the theory was only a chapter in his monumental *Histoire de la literature anglaise*, and the model was inspired by a scientific (biological) parallel, viz. the growth of a tree. Incidentally, Taine's three criteria did not, in his own view, supply a complete explanation, so he had to add a fourth condition, viz. *la faculté maîtresse*, which was supposed to account for the contribution made by the author's talent or genius. That supplement was indirect evidence, supported by many "humanistic" contemporaries, that the scientific idiom was incapable of accounting for everything.

In fact, most prominent men of letters were engaged in a fierce struggle about values, a confrontation that tended to become more and more intransigent from the middle of the 19th century onwards. Men like Stuart Mill, Ruskin, and Pater, and certainly also Arnold, were seriously worried and genuinely frightened by the relentless progress of science, which they saw as a mixture of crass materialism and provocative godlessness. Arnold's ideas about 'seeing the object as it really is' and 'disinterestedness' in criticism are not only a response to the Romanticists' paddling their own canoe, but also an attempt to apply verifiable criteria to a non-scientific object. Arnold and his kindred spirits took up the cudgels for a 'non-materialistic' cause in the fields of philosophy, politics, and religion, and literature was used deliberately as a weapon in the campaign.

The Oxford Movement, which was initiated by a sermon by Keple in 1833, aimed at reviving a higher conception than was generally prevalent of the position and functions of the Church as 'more than a mainly human institution', and possessing sacraments ultimately ordained by Christ. Though later disrupted and eventually broken up, the Movement's energetic resistance to scientific method, and its emphasis on the message had a considerable impact from the middle of the century.

The naturalist Charles Darwin was not the only writer who was interested in origins. Philosophers and critics began to excogitate solutions to the problem of how literary works came into being. Earlier than Taine, Sainte-Beuve was a spokesman for the postulate that a cause-effect relationship existed between a writer's biography and his literary output: the work was taken to be the product if its author's 'ererbt, erlebt, erlernt', i.e. largely measurable phenomena. Some people – be they factual or fictitious – were privileged in the sense that their *curriculum vitae* was more worth recording than that of others. It was not a question of subtle psychological operators; psychology as a scientific research area was a later conquest, and Victorian Positivists were highly suspicious of introspection.

The mechanical correspondence between background and conduct is visible in many contemporary novels, in which items of 'biographical' information are provided before an important character enters the stage. A case in point is Miss Havisham in *Great Expectations*; or think of the elaborate introductory pages in Balzac's novels, for example. *Le Père Goriot*, where the neighbourhood, the street, the house and the rooms are meticulously detailed before the main character makes his appearance and turns out to be a function of his environment. Incidentally, Dr Johnson called his evaluative essays *Lives of the Poets*.

The purpose was to brief the reader and tell him what kind of conduct he might expect on the part of the character or characters. An analogous procedure was followed by George Bernard Shaw in his elaborate stage directions. But the aim was also to reassure the reader that the way had been properly paved and the scene carefully set for the plot to take its start.

The 'correspondence theory' is another illustration of the mechanical explanation of things that came to prevail as the 19th century progressed. Though Arnold was highly sceptical of the tendency and combated it nail and tooth throughout his life, he followed the pattern established by a contemporary critic like Sainte-Beuve, whose name he mentions on several occasions, in the structure of many of his essays.

The Zeitgeist being what it was, it comes as no surprise that formal considerations should be pushed into the background, or simply be ignored. At the most, such observations were reduced to vacuous value judgements. It took radical breaches of the formal decorum, which was felt to exist in spite of the fact that it was never clearly formulated, to raise contemporary hackles; that is what Clough did with his hexameters.

Arnold had a high opinion of poetry and of literature generally. In his Inauguration Lecture as Professor at Oxford University (1857) he claimed that the poetry (by which he probably means literature) of an age provides the noblest representation of that age. And he was not talking of elegant metaphors or sophisticated verse patterns.

Analysing Arnold as a *literary* critic is a challenge beset with difficulties. Disentangling the components that go into his idea of criticism is no easy job, not least because he would not have dreamt of doing it himself.

CHAPTER TWO

THE LETTERS OF MATTHEW ARNOLD TO ARTHUR HUGH CLOUGH

The Strayed Reveller, Arnold's first volume of poetry, contained two poems, *To a Friend* and *To a Republican Friend*. The friend is Arthur Hugh Clough.

The two men became friends at Rugby, where Thomas Arnold, Matthew's father was headmaster. Clough was one of Thomas Arnold's favourite pupils, highly gifted and extremely conscientious. He won the friendship of many fellow students and was in his youth a promising poet and critic. However, much to everybody's surprise, he underperformed when he was in his twenties, and he barely managed to become a fellow at Oriel. Matthew Arnold admired Clough, who was three years his senior, and perhaps envied him a little because he was "high-spirited, deeply imaginative, and full of gusto".[1] Also, the two men shared a love of poetry and of the practice of it.

Clough died suddenly and prematurely in 1861, at the age of 42. In spite of his warm feelings for his friend, Arnold, like many contemporaries, thought that Clough had never really lived up to their expectations, and Arnold was fully aware that in *Thyrsis*, his elegy on Clough, which was finished four years after the latter's death, he gave an idealized picture of his friend.

"I am forever linked with you by intellectual bonds – the strongest of all," Arnold wrote to Clough in 1853.[2] The two men loved to discuss poetry, and in Arnold's letters to Clough from the late 1840s and onwards until the latter's death, Arnold tested many of his ideas of what poetry "ought to be".

In the letters Arnold wrote to his friend from 1847 and until the publication of the *Preface* in 1853, are found numerous intimations of what was to be the supporting pillars of the *Preface*, reflections that we meet again and again also in Arnold's later essays. To some extent, Arnold used the correspondence to advance his own views in combination with cautious and tactful criticism of Clough's poems. Arnold performs a veritable egg dance in that he constantly encourages Clough and finds details to praise in his verse, yet never conceals the fact that he finds Clough's poems defective: on March 6, 1848, he commends the poems for their "wide and deep-spread intelligence".[3] However, in mid-December 1847, his comment runs as follows: "I have abstained from all general criticism . . . The 2nd poem . . . I do not think valuable – worthy of you – what is the word?"[4]

It was not least Clough's soaring ambition about "solving the Universe" that aroused Arnold's scepticism. Still, "reconstructing" it is not satisfactory either. But perhaps "unsatisfactoriness is the aim of poetry," Arnold adds.[5]

Arnold was perfectly candid about the quality of his own poems: he is aware of what he considers their "imperfection", but he doubts that he will ever have sufficient "heat and radiance . . . to pierce the clouds that are massed around me", he writes in December 1852.[6] And in May 1853, a few months before the publication of the *Preface*, he writes:

"I feel immensely – more and more clearly – what I *want* – what I have (I believe) lost and choked by my treatment of myself, and the studies to which I have addicted myself. But what ought I to have done in preference to what I have done? there is the question."[7]

That self-reproach can be read as a reflection on the easy-going way in which he spent several of his formative years – actually his family were surprised to see the seriousness of his first collection of poems. The statement sounds like a deep sigh from a person standing on the threshold of a more serious and demanding adult existence, who is beginning to settle his accounts, but has not yet found his bearings.

It is difficult to take Arnold's statement about the way he went about his studies seriously – witness the erudition of his *Preface*, but the attitude does explain Arnold's insistent wish for a standard to regulate the writing of poetry, and it also contains a clue to his frequently expressed admiration for French and German writers in his essays. In his letters to Clough, he pays tribute to both Goethe and Novalis, and the *Preface* breathes uncritical respect for "the Ancients", more particularly the Greek tragedians.

Modern poetry can only "subsist by its *contents*," he writes on October 28, 1852 (his italics), "by becoming a complete *magister vitae*, as the poetry of the ancients did; by including, as theirs did, religion with poetry, instead of existing as poetry only, and leaving religious wants to be supplied by the Christian religion, as a power of existing independent of the poetical power."[8] The idea of poetry's inability to "stand alone" rests with Arnold during his whole life.

That is why Keats and Shelley were wrong when "trying to imitate Elizabethan exuberance of expression, charm, richness of images . . . ."[9] Especially Keats comes in for more persistent and relentless scorn, in these letters as well as in the *Preface*: "passionately desiring movement and fullness, and obtaining but a confused multitudinousness."[10]

As Arnold saw it – and as he repeated in the *Preface* – Keats, "a style and form seeker," was fundamentally wrong: the aim of poetry is not "to produce exquisite bits and images", though Arnold reluctantly admits that some of Keats' formulations are extremely successful. The language of poetry should be very plain, direct and severe; and it must not lose itself in parts and episodes and ornamental work, but must press forward to the whole" (October 28, 1852).[11]

It would not seem an unwarranted conjecture that Arnold's life-long obsession with wholes at the expense of parts had its origin in his literary studies. In the Greek tragedies he found a number of integrated works of art whose *architectonicè* permitted them to teach a moral. Arnold transferred the Greek example to his social and theological thinking: parts were divisive, leading to disruption and potential chaos. For example, Chapter IV of *Culture and Anarchy*, written in 1868, a year of turbulence at home and abroad, is devoted to a lengthy warning against the disestablishment of the Irish Church.[12]

"Multitudinousness" is a word that arouses Arnold's suspicion.[13] "Trying to go into and to the bottom of an object instead of grouping *objects* is as fatal to the seriousness of poetry as the mere painting . . . is to its airy and moving life" (his italics).[14] "Mere painting" and "go to the bottom of an object" are jibes not only at one of his pet aversions, viz. the Romantic poets' excessive use of imagery, it also exposes the technique of science, which Arnold held in contempt.

The concept of synthesis also determines Arnold's reflections on the way poetry is created: a poet "must begin with an Idea of the world in order not to be prevailed over by the world's multitudinousness: or if they cannot get that, at least with isolated ideas: and all other things shall (perhaps) be added unto them" (September 1848–49).[15]

So, the poet must have a total conception, which serves as a generator of the creative process, and "the rest" – for example the structuring – will "perhaps" follow. The source of inspiration is to be found in an existing body of criticism, as Arnold was later to emphasize, and the writing of poetry becomes a deductive process. Arnold's later socially and theologically tinted essays also have an overall idea as their starting-point.

Poetry to Arnold is a didactic enterprise. There are two "offices of poetry – one to add to one's store of thoughts and feelings, another to compose and elevate the mind by a sustained tone, numerous allusions, and a grand style", he writes on March 1, 1849.[16] What that boils down to is that both the content and the form should be edifying, and that, to Arnold, is a necessary prerequisite for poetry being pleasurable.

One of the maxims that followed Arnold throughout his life is that poetry is a criticism of life. Accordingly, a great subject is vital, and that was where "those d__d Elizabethan poets generally" went disastrously wrong".[17] "As far as you can, choose *adequate subjects* and put your mark on them (July 27, 1853) (his italics).[18]

As far as style is concerned, Arnold is ambivalent: "For the style is the expression of the nobility of the poet's character, as the matter is the expression of the richness of is mind; but on men, character produces as great an effect as mind" (March 1, 1849).[19] The formulation might seem to indicate parity of esteem for form and content. However, other letters show that there is a difference: in a letter dated early February 1849 we read: "Form of conception comes by nature certainly, but is generally developed late; but this lower form of expression is found from the beginning amongst all born poets, even feeble thinkers, and in an unpoetical age; as Collins, Greene [he probably means Gray] and fifty more in England only."[20]

Handling the structure of a piece of writing seems to be a pretty simple affair. That is perhaps one of the reasons why novelists and the art of the novel did not command respect in Arnold's reflections. In the *Preface*, which is, to all intents and purposes, a rudimentary theory of literature rather than an introduction to some poems, there are no references at all to novels or novelists, and in the letters to Clough, there are two off-hand value judgements, seemingly meant to serve only as bits of information: on March 21, 1853, Arnold characterizes Charlotte Brontë's *Villette* as "one of the most utterly disagreeable books I ever read."[21] In the same letter, Thackeray's *Henry Esmond* is awarded more generous, but still superficial, praise:

"It is one of the most readable books I ever met. Thackeray is a first-rate journeyman, though not a great artist."

Most of the large number of letters that Arnold wrote to Clough from the mid-forties to the latter's death in 1862 are of a diary-like character. Their content is what would today be recorded in an e-mail. However, some of them are relevant for the subject of this book. They show to what extent Arnold had developed his theoretical reflections on poetry when he was in his mid-twenties. They appear as appendices to, or conclusions of, Arnold's evaluations of Clough's literary achievements, and they are more than mere tentative or groping suggestions. By this time, Arnold has some indisputable views on the aims of poetry, the task of the poet, the respect due to the ancient Greeks, and the weighing up of the roles of form and content in a literary work.

Arnold gives no sources – after all, the letters are personal exchanges between friends. But they express views that we meet in an elaborated, but essentially unchanged, form in the *Preface*. No less interesting is the tone adopted by Arnold: the raised forefinger is symptomatic of the way he would always address his readers. Arnold speaks here and elsewhere as the teacher – benign, persuasive, appealing to the reader's common sense, and never for a moment doubting the obviousness of his own opinions. Clough is treated as the neophyte who, admittedly, has some shortcomings, but who, on the other hand, shows the will as well as the capacity to learn. The teacher shows confidence in his pupil.

Arnold's approach is as pedagogic as that of a competent teacher: he apportions blame and praise scrupulously; his advice is cautious, but unmistakable. However, judging from the late letters of the correspondence, Clough did not heed Arnold's words. Arnold hides his surprise – or irritation – behind a veil of affable tactfulness, but between the lines it is not difficult to discern a slight disappointment. And contemporary critics shared Arnold's reservations and gentle wonder vis-à-vis the somewhat fanciful output of a man who seemed to them to misuse his talent. Clough was a fervent believer, which Arnold of course saw as an asset, and which may have been one of the bases of their friendship.

CHAPTER THREE

THE *PREFACE* OF 1853

Summary

The *Preface* begins by stating that the poem *Empedocles on Etna* has been left out of the collection. The reason, viz. that the poem is painful, but not tragic, is given a bit later in the text (xvii).[1] Gradually the reader is led into an account of the task of poetry and of the poet, which naturally merges into a description of the demands to be met by the content of poetry for it to give pleasure to the reader. Next follows an elaborate defence of the ancient Greeks, which turns out to be one of the cornerstones of the text: the Greeks ought to determine the choice of subject (xix) because they had an acknowledged theory which differs from the modern one, and they mastered the control of form. Arnold maintains the tone of respectful awe towards the Ancients throughout: they understood how to give the right proportion to wholes and parts – be the latter ever so brilliant (xxiii) – and they avoided the Romantic poets' besetting sin, viz. effusiveness (xxiv). Keats' poem *Isabella* is singled out for special treatment as an unfortunate example (xxvi), but even Shakespeare – although awarded polite acknowledgement – causes Arnold to raise his eyebrows: Arnold would like more matter, less words.

The reservations Arnold has to make about the Ancients are few and insignificant, and the *Preface* ends with an injunction on contemporary poets to strive to write works of eternal interest. That invitation partly excludes the poets' own age for the choice of an appropriate subject. However, the works of the Ancients – in the text, reference has been made mainly to the Greek tragedies, more particularly those of Sophocles – have proved to have universal value.

Subject

The choice of the correct 'object' (by which Arnold means subject) of poetry is crucial. For a poem to be perfect, it must have a perfect subject. Interestingly, Arnold shows no similar concern about what creates a formally perfect poem. As Arnold sees it, "human action . . . communicated in an interesting manner by the poet" (xix) holds an appeal to "the great primary human affections", among which Arnold reckons passion and suffering (xx). However, those two must be implemented in action. Depicting situations "in which suffering finds no vent in action" will provide no pleasure. And "no poetical enjoyment can be derived" from the kind of suffering "in which a continuous state of mental stress is prolonged" (xviii).

At this point of the *Preface*, Arnold seems to consider both sides of the Horatian diptych, *prodesse et delectare*. However, as the text goes along, it becomes evident that Arnold has a specific kind of pleasure in mind, viz the satisfaction that stems from edifying instruction and from problems being solved in terms of action. That which is great and passionate is "eternally interesting" and, Arnold implies, didactic. Nowhere in the text does Arnold outline a background against which the "action" is to be performed, and nowhere is a possible or desirable result sketched out. That is the more regrettable since, apparently, not any action will do. As evidenced by his later writings, Arnold did not speak up for revolutionary uprising or patriotic struggles for freedom. Arnold was a decidedly peaceable man who nowhere in his prose shows any awareness of the implications of the upheaval that was taking place right under his nose, but was genuinely upset by some people trespassing into a fenced-off park. Characteristically, the "action" idea is perceptibly toned down in Arnold's later discussions of appropriate subjects for poetry.

Actually, the ancient Greeks had made the ideal choice of subjects in that they managed to establish a link between "great primary human affections" and "action". Apparently, Arnold did not object to the narrow range of subjects treated by the Greek dramatists. What mattered to the humanist Arnold was that neither steam engines nor factories appear in Sophocles' plays. Scientific progress and the great achievements of industrial development and social amelioration cannot furnish suitable subjects because Arnold's own age lacks "moral grandeur" and suffers from "spiritual discomfort" (xix).

The choice of subject is significant for another reason: in Arnold's opinion, each theme has its own appropriate form, and the style of a work "draws its force directly from the pregnancy of the matter it conveys" (xxi). (*OED* records meanings like 'fertility', 'productiveness', imaginative power' for 'pregnancy'.) The statement is not without some justification: Racine's plays, about which Arnold has, surprisingly, nothing at all to say, are cut to a certain fixed pattern and could not have been written as comedies, and elegies have a style of their own. Probably, a snide comment on the undisciplined Romantics is also intended here. And Arnold has another point to make: since the problem at issue is, ideally speaking, one of "perennial" interest, the dating of the action depicted becomes, in principle, irrelevant (xxii). Here, Arnold has to beat about the bush: a contemporary subject is perhaps "too near" a modern poet. By the same token, it may be too difficult for a modern poet to "know the externals of a past action . . . with the passion of a contemporary" (xxi). But that only applies to "the outward man", e.g. "the house in which they lived" and not with "the inward man", his "feelings and behaviour in certain tragic situations . . . these have in them nothing local and casual" (xxi). So, a foggy formulation spirits away the problem, and at the same time, the Romantics, with their privately inspired sentimentality, are put in their place.

The Poet's Task

What the poet's task actually amounts to in Arnold's perception is hard to unravel. The poet is supposed to choose a subject from among a variety of possibilities, almost like a customer in a supermarket picking from the shelves the items that he likes best. Selection is all-important, and the poet ought to choose an action that appeals to "the great primary human affections" (xx), which are, however, never itemized.

Arnold repeatedly talks about "raw action", which seems to mean action conveyed by the poet without any paraphernalia. Yet it is inconceivable that a mere report would suffice. There are some loose ends to be tied up here. On the one hand, Arnold claims that construction is "all-important": it was so to the Greeks, and it ought to be so to us. For example, if the Athenian spectators, of whose mind-set Arnold claims to have both knowledge and understanding, were familiar with the plot dramatized on the stage, surely the processing of the dramatist is of vital importance for the way the audience would "be incited and rejoice"?

On the other hand, the "noble action" should "subsist as it did in nature" (xxiii). However, if the "raw action" is left more or less in its virgin state, how can it become a work of art? When Arnold states (xxix) that poets should write about "great actions calculated powerfully to affect what is permanent in the human soul", the 'what' is left hanging in the air, but the formulation ("calculated") makes it plausible that some activity on the poet's part is requisite.

And Arnold does presuppose active contribution from the poet: his task is to give his readers "the highest pleasure which they are capable of feeling" (xix), and one of the basic assumptions of the *Preface* is that the authors of Arnold's own age will hardly be capable of providing such pleasure.

Poetry should give pleasure to the reader. However, Arnold is at pains to emphasize that it is the reader's poetical rather than his rhetorical sense that poets ought to "gratify" (xxiii). That is another way of formulating the common thread that runs through all Arnold's written work, viz. that content is more important than form.

Arnold gives no examples of a poet who has met his criteria – the absence of concrete exemplification is a characteristic of all that Arnold wrote. There is a reference to Goethe and – rather unexpectedly – to Niebuhr, but the two men are called in testify to the deplorable state of things in Arnold's own age. It should be added that, in his later work, Arnold conceives of Goethe primarily as a critic.

"Contemplation of some noble action of a heroic time" (xxix) would be desirable, but that is the preserve of the chosen few who have absorbed the Classics. They are able to talk freely and without "the delirium of vanity" about their moralizing mission. Thus, with effortless ease, the Classics are harnessed to Arnold's own preferences.

Arnold's mantra of "a noble action" crops up again towards the end of the *Preface*: genuine artists will penetrate themselves with some noble action, a fact that will prevent them from indulging in panegyric enthusiasm for their own age. Poets should rather search for elements that will "affect what is permanent in the human soul" (xxix)

The poet should not go out of his way to devise interesting formal structures. No, the poet should "efface himself" and "enable a noble action to subsist as it did in nature" (xxiii). On the other hand, the poet's intuitive handling should be different from that of a mere reporter. Accordingly, a young poet needs "a hand to guide him" (xxiv), and since no established authority exists in the form of an institution, the young poet's attention should be directed towards models (xxiv). For the act of writing poetry can be learned, and, like the Neo-Classicists before him,

Arnold advises neophytes to imitate the Ancients; Arnold mentions Sophocles as an appropriate model.

In the final paragraphs of the *Preface*, Arnold, hiding behind his revered mentor, Goethe, warns poets not to go to extremes. It will not do for a poet to neglect "the indispensable part" (whatever that may be!) and think he has done enough if he shows "spirituality and feeling" (xxx). And they who seek to arrive at the stage of poetry merely by "mechanism . . . in which they can acquire an artisan's readiness", will end up "without soul and matter" (xxx). Such types are characterized as *dilettanti*, and they are, we understand, radically different from genuine poets who have drunk deep of the Pierian spring. But, once more, Arnold climbs down: that does not justify heaping scorn upon them. Thus Arnold ends his *Preface* on a note of conciliatory obligingness – his preferred stance in most of what he committed to paper.

Creation

Arnold makes light of the creative process: "this done" (i.e. choosing a proper subject), "everything else will follow" (xxiii). The idea is identical with the one propounded by Cato the Elder in his advice to orators: "rem tene, verba sequentur". Arnold quotes a remark by Menander to illustrate a perfect creative situation: when somebody "inquired as to the progress of his comedy", Menander answered that "he had finished it, not having written a single line because he had constructed the action of it in his mind" (xxiii). That intuitive approach is preferable to a working method based on stepwise progression, in which a poet would write down "the brilliant things which arose under his pen as he went along" (xxiii). The postulate is not very Informative, but it chimes in very well with Arnold's repeated preference of wholes to parts, intuition being the situation in which a person senses a whole without being cognizant of the parts that went into it.

Arnold attributed a huge importance to criticism, which he considered the origin of poetic creation. Therefore, he is worried about the "confusion of the present time" within literary criticism. His indignation is aroused by contemporary critics who extol poets for giving "a free allegory of their own minds". That procedure will never lead to the creation of great poetry. For once, Arnold gives a concrete example: even though he admired Goethe as a critic, he found *Faust* unsatisfactory.

Models: Classics and Moderns, Shakespeare, Representation, Part and Wholes

Classics and Moderns

Arnold received a solid classical grounding at Rugby, the school where his father was headmaster.[2]

Throughout his life, Arnold preserved a reverential and enthusiastic attitude to what he called the Ancients. However, his use of that term is rather narrow. For one thing, it does not include Latin authors and critics like Horace and Vergil, who were, by many of Arnold's predecessors, affirmed to have established standard of permanent validity worth striving to achieve or at least emulate. Actually, Horace's *Ars poetica* was for centuries read like the fifth gospel, but Arnold never mentions Horace in his critical oeuvre, and he has only a few passing references to Vergil.

To Arnold, "the Ancients" were synonymous with the *Poetics* of Aristotle plus the Greek tragedians, more particularly the dramas of Sophocles, and Homer's epics. He was charmed by Homer's "rapidity of movement, plainness in words and style, simplicity of ideas, and nobility of manner."[3] Arnold studied Homer throughout his life, and he saw Homer as a challenging object of translation, which is proved by the title of one of his essays, *On Translating Homer* (1861).

The tragic vision embodied in the dramas of Sophocles found an echo in Arnold's attitude to life, which he saw it incumbent on poetry (by which he often means literature) to verbalize. The moral expounded by Sophocles, viz. that man reaches nobility through the performance of some bold and tragic action which inevitably caused suffering and eventually loss of life, was entirely to Arnold's taste.[4] The Greeks called the ensuing reaction among the spectator catharsis, and they considered the combination of pity and fear healthy as well as pleasurable. That conception of pleasure was endorsed whole-heartedly by Arnold, who, perhaps unwittingly twisting the Horatian maxim *prodesse et delectare*, saw it as the task of poetry to "inspirit and rejoice" the reader (xviii).

From the outset, Arnold steers his course by the Ancients, more particularly by the doctrines laid down by Aristotle in his *Poetics*. Most of the material of the *Preface* consists of quotations from, and gentle applications of, the deductions made by the Stagyrite on the basis of the dramas of the great tragedians. Arnold seemingly forgets that he is writing an introduction to a collection of poems. It would not be misleading to call the *Preface* Arnold's recipe for a perfect tragedy.

In Arnold's opinion, the Greek dramatists did the right thing when they sought their themes in a distant past. He never comments on the fact that Sophocles and his fellow dramatists took their material from myths. Arnold preferred serious subjects, and contemporary themes (unspecified) are relegated to the "lighter kinds of poetry" and to comedy (xx and xxii). Such themes are inappropriate for what Arnold calls *pragmatic* poetry, which means serious poetry (xxii; his italics).

To bring home his point, Arnold juxtaposes specimens from "the Greek stage" and the modern "domestic epic like *Hermann and Dorothea*" (xx) and "the episode of Dido" and "Childe Harold", and of course his verdict is a foregone conclusion.

It is a sign of the surprisingly selective frame of reference of the *Preface* that, in his search for post-classical authors worthy to serve as models, Arnold should overlook Racine. Arnold was a declared Francophile, well versed in French literature and culture, witness the inspiration he drew from Sainte-Beuve.

Racine treated the same subjects as Arnold's beloved Greek ideals, and his tragedies had the wholeness that Arnold never tired of setting up as an ideal. On page xxvii of the *Preface*, Arnold calls for "clearness of arrangement, rigorous development, simplicity of style", which reads like a declaration of content for a Racinian tragedy.

One would also have thought that the social circumstances in which Arnold and his contemporaries found themselves might have furnished ample material for tragedies with heroes and villains of Sophoclean dimensions. Such blind spots testify to the surprising and disappointing narrowness of outlook that is also evident in Arnold's later essays.

Literature ought to deal with man's "feelings and behaviour in certain tragic situations" (xxii). Tragic situations, Arnold postulates, are particularly suitable to arouse pleasure, provided that the situation be implemented in action. The incidents portrayed must show resistance and hope. What the Greek tragedians teach us is that man must grapple with the calamities of life (xxiii), even at the cost of his own life. Such a sequence of events is sure to give the readers or spectators a sense of relief. A modern poet would be wise to "delight himself with the contemplation of some noble action" (xxx), and in that respect the Greeks are unsurpassed masters.

Well into the *Preface*, we are told that the poem *Empedocles on Etna* was omitted from the collection because it was "poetically faulty" (xxviii). The poet-philosopher Empedocles lived in a time of incipient unrest, and Arnold discovered, in that period, a decline of "the calm, the cheerfulness, the disinterested objectivity" (xvii), a fact that made a person like Empedocles less appropriate as the protagonist of a poem. For a brief moment, Arnold seems to have forgotten the pervasive homage paid to action in the *Preface*. But the elaborate beating about the bush that we witness in the opening pages of the *Preface* to account for the omission of *Empedocles on Etna* actually serves as a foil to introduce the reader to one of the purposes of Arnold's text, viz. to set out his ideals for poetry.

Arnold has no qualms about using action as the centrepiece of a poem. However, it is something of a paradox that Arnold, who in his essays appears as the level-headed middle-of-the-road person and who advocates common sense and rational argumentation, should, at this time be an uncompromising adherent of action in poetry.

Arnold pursues the centuries old idea that the writing of poetry is a craft that can be learned. For aspiring poets to be properly taught, Arnold held, it would be necessary for them to have some models to imitate, and with their inherent qualities, the Greeks would be eminently suitable. Modern poets can learn three things from the Ancients: "choice of *subject*, accurate *construction* and the subordinate character of *expression*" (xxviii; his italics). This goes hand in hand with Arnold's warning to young poets not to be "impressed by their own age" (xxix).

Those reflections, illustrating Arnold's life-long scepticism vis-à-vis his own age, lead up to the establishment of a contrast between the eternal and the transitory. Arnold has no doubt that the Ancients have come closer to the everlasting truths, and since the aim of young poets, according to Arnold, should be to produce immortal masterpieces, the transitory nature of much that is modern is of no avail to them. Arnold's implication is that only great themes are capable of engaging man's deepest and noblest feelings. The claims of "the transient feelings and passions of their own present age are to be directed elsewhere" (xx). The works of modern poets should keep within the frames mapped out by the Ancients, even though Arnold is prepared to admit that their choice of subjects may sometimes be somewhat restricted.

What also captivates Arnold is that "on the Greek tragic stage" in its prime there was consensus between authors and critics because the dramatists knew what to do with their art, viz."unity and profundity of moral impression" (xxviii). A modern reader will tend to think that the consensus is not difficult to explain: little Greek dramatic criticism apart from the *Poetics* of Aristotle is extant, and that work is, to all intents and purposes, a list of deductions from the procedure of actually existing and repeatedly performed plays. But the consensus idea conforms to the suave sweetness-and-light pattern that is a thread running through Arnoldian criticism.

Shakespeare

Whereas the Greek dramatists would serve as perfect models for fledgling poets, the case of Shakespeare is more dubious (xxiv). With his usual effort to strike a balance, Arnold goes out of his way to be fair to the Bard. He is obviously uncomfortable at having to push him off the pedestal, but on the other hand he feels duty-bound to state that Shakespeare lacked the "purity of method" to be found in the Ancients (xxvii) though, admittedly, he did have their "excellent action" (xxvi). Shakespeare is absolved from guilt on some of Arnold's cardinal points: he chose his subjects from the past, and his plays are not primarily about his own state of mind. The highest praise Arnold can award to him is that in many respects he resembles the Ancients (xxvii) – he was even possessed of a richer fertility of thought than they were. Yet he did not have the restraint of the Ancients, his wholes are defective, and his language is sometimes difficult to understand.

But, worst of all, Shakespeare's linguistic brilliance blurs the moral issue, and his harmful influence is visible in the poetry of John Keats. Arnold recognizes Keats' poetic stature, but he gives a scathing comment on the latter's poem *Isabella*. It is evidence, says Arnold that even a great poet's skill cannot vitalize a "small" subject (xx).

Keats was chosen as the scapegoat, but actually Arnold was sceptical of all the Romantic poets. One of the purposes of the *Preface* is to give vent to Arnold's disgust at the Romantic idiom, which he found shallow and dangerously escapist. The Romantic poets were the antipodes of the Greek tragedians. Arnold found the view of "the modern critic" (who is not given a name) misguided when he states that "a true allegory of the state of one's own mind in a representative history is perhaps the highest thing that one can attempt in the way of poetry" (xxiii–xxiv). Arnold was genuinely alarmed at what he saw as the Romantic poets' uninhibited gushing forth of their own emotions – his headshake is audible and occurs repeatedly later in his essays. The relentless and uncontrollable machinery of *Oedipus* was a more appropriate subject than the west wind or Kubla Khan. Not that introspection as such was despicable, though. Again, the reader cannot help being baffled by the unpredictability and inconsistency of the stance adopted by Arnold. In his later, morally tinted essays, Arnold repeatedly underlines the advisability of "looking inwards in order to find one's "true self" and cultivate it.

It is a well-known fact that, with his tragedy *Merope* Arnold attempted to show his contemporaries what a tragedy ought to be. However, the play was a miserable failure ("unreadable", said Chambers), and in spite of Arnold's untiring efforts to persuade theatre managers to give it a chance, the play sank into oblivion. So, in that case there was no felicitous consensus between a dramatist and his critics.

Representation

On the very first page of the *Preface*, Arnold quotes with approval Aristotle's reflections on imitation and representations, which are taken from the latter's chapter on tragedy[5]. The representation aspect, which in Aristotle covers the performance, is used by Arnold in the sense of composition and style. All Arnold says in that respect is that "every representation, therefore, which is consistently drawn, may be supposed to be interesting" (xvii). One detects the idea of *architectonicè* behind that formulation, but it also shows that the dress of the thought should cater for the interests of the reader. But the fact that he stressed the message aspect of a text meant that Arnold relegated the form of a work to a decidedly inferior position. Thus, Aristotle's detailed discussion of "diction" in Sections xxv and xv of *Poetics*[6] is entirely ignored by Arnold. What is essential to him is that the representation is successful – if not, the work forfeits its august purpose. It is the action treated as a whole that leaves "the one moral impression". The choice of the word representation, a term from the world of the drama, about the form of a poem, is more evidence of the terminological vacillation of the *Preface*.

"We should not admire the Greeks uncritically" (xxvii). Yet, Arnold's reservations, such as they are, are couched in cautious, almost reluctant terms: the Ancients may be less suggestive than Shakespeare, and Antigone's dilemma may seem too narrow, but such weaknesses are more than compensated for by the overall "instructiveness".

Arnold raises his forefinger at "the jargon of modern criticism", which encourages the composition of works "conceived in the spirit of the passing time" (xxviii). Yet, there are some rays of comfort in the midst of the general gloom: Schiller is praised for his message of joy, and Goethe, whom Arnold admired as "the greatest critic of our own age", is complimented for sharing Arnold's attitude to his own age (xxiv). However, regrettably, Goethe's dramatic oeuvre does not distinguish itself by sufficient action, though, of course, Arnold hastens to add, the theme of *Faust* is a perennial one.

Unexpectedly, Carsten Niebuhr is also admitted to the fold of *les acceptables*. That Danish-born orientalist was anything but a literary critic, but he was internationally *en vogue* in the former half of the 19th century, perhaps because of his love of adventure and his exotic accounts of his travels[7]. He died in 1815 and can hardly be recognized as belonging to Arnold's "present age", and neither here nor in his later essays does Arnold reveal any profound knowledge of him. In the *Preface* he only appears as an instance of names-dropping.

Towards the end of the *Preface*, Arnold attempts to smooth away some of his pronounced animosity against his own age: we should not adopt a "hostile attitude to it, but just be careful not to be overwhelmed" by its "false pretentions". But in the question of "what is sound and true in poetical art, I seemed to myself to find the only guidance, the only solid footing, among the ancients" (xxx). By now, Arnold is almost euphoric: "commerce with the ancients" seems to have "a steadying and composing effect" on those who practise it (xxviii). Their judgement, not of literary works only, but of "men and events in general" (xxviii) is better balanced, and they are "more truly than others under the empire of facts", and they "wish to know what it (sc. their age) is" (xxviii), a statement which is in perfect accordance with one of his maxims that Arnold repeats *ad nauseam*, viz. "seeing things as they are.". Besides, such people want to "cultivate what is best and noblest in themselves" (xxviii). That type of introspection-cum-moralizing is another of Arnold's great ideas.

The *Preface* ends with a typically Arnoldian middle-of-the-road quotation from Goethe to the effect that we should avoid stressing either form or content unduly (a point that goes against most of the statements in the *Preface*). The essential thing is that we "have so much respect for our Art as to prefer it to ourselves" (xxx) – the devoted artist sacrificing himself on the altar of his art.

Parts and Wholes

In *Poetics*, Part III, Section 1, *Of the Epic Poem*, Aristotle writes: "It is obvious that the fable ought to be dramatically constructed like that of a tragedy; and that it should have for its subject one entire and perfect action, having a beginning, a middle and an end; so that, forming like an animal a complete whole, it may afford its proper pleasure . . . ".[8]

Aristotle talks about epic poems, and the rules he lays down for them are almost identical with those that he established for tragedy. Arnold adopted unquestioningly Aristotle's demand for a poem to be an organic whole. What matters to Arnold is the total structure of a literary work from which a moral is easily deducible. The strength of the Greeks' poetic theory and practice, as Arnold saw it, is that they prefer wholes to parts, unlike modern authors who spend a considerable amount of energy creating beautiful details.

Architectonicè is one of Arnold's favourite concepts, which he inherited from Goethe, and which says that wholeness is all. That idea is naturally linked to Arnold's avowed enthusiasm for large, harmonious and illuminating syntheses when he deals with political, social, or religious issues. As was pointed out earler,[9] it is certainly surprising, in the light of Arnold's concern with large-scale structures that, not only in the 1853 *Preface*, but also in the many literary essays that he wrote later, he should show virtually no interest in contemporary novelists' technique.

Arnold's life-long interest in French literature began in his early youth. By the time the *Preface* was written, Balzac had published several seminal novels (thus *Le Pére Goriot* in 1834), and on English soil Dickens' *David Copperfield* appeared in 1849–50, and Thackeray's *Vanity Fair* in 1847. Novels were beginning to make an impact not only in literary circles, and they satisfied at least two of Aristotle's conditions: they were integrated wholes with a beginning, a middle, and an end, and they embodied a moral. Contemporary evidence shows that they gave pleasure to quite a lot of readers. Arnold's grievance against novels, whose social criticism would seem to be palatable to him, was probably that they did not present "one entire and perfect action," containing, as they did, secondary and convoluted plots and seemingly irrelevant digressions. The danger was that the didactic element might be thrown to the winds, and *architectonicè* thus marred.

Arnold does not object to parts *per se*, provided they form a synthesis. However, "occasional bursts of fine writing" (xxiii) do not suffice. A simple successful line or a short mellifluous passage cannot have the same impact as a whole that breathes instruction. Arnold advances the postulate that profundity of single thoughts, richness of imagery and abundance of illustration are easy to learn, witness the works of "modern writers." He finds it disastrous if a reader, after finishing a work, should exclaim about the author, "il dit tout ce qu'il veut, mais malheureusement il n'a rien à dire" (xxv).

Arnold does not operate with the division of literature into genres, so *architectonicè* is to him a cross-genre valid criterion of success. Even if the term suggests construction and planning, Arnold never spends a word on the building blocks that are required to create the synthesis. On the contrary he uses a kind of negative argumentation by attempting to prove that undue emphasis on particularities will invariably yield deplorable results.

His guinea pigs are the Romantic poets, especially Keats, and, to some extent, Shakespeare. Using his usual tactics of diversionary manoeuvring, Arnold begins by lauding Keats' exquisite genius, and he admits that, for example, *Isabella or the Pot of Basil* abounds with graceful and felicitous images – indeed, the poem contains more single happy expressions than all of Sophocles' dramas put together (xxvi). However, although "the action in itself is an excellent one" (xxvi), it is so "feebly conceived and loosely constructed" that "the effect produced by it . . . is absolutely null" (xxvi). And *Endymion* is denounced for being "utterly incoherent", i.e. lacking wholeness.

The passage illustrates how many sins Keats has on his conscience: single lines may shine, but coherence is missing; a promising action is bungled, and the total construction is a failure. There is here and elsewhere an undertone of annoyance with Keats for wasting his obvious talent, which means not using it for the purposes Arnold could approve of.

However, Arnold had bigger fish to fry. Also Shakespeare is weighed and found wanting in several respects. Shakespeare receives a pat on the shoulder for his talent of conceiving an action and grasping a situation and for "his power . . . of intimately associating himself with a character" (xxvi). Arnold goes so far as to admit that Shakespeare no doubt possessed "the fundamental excellences of poetical art" (xxvi), and that he had "a gift . . . of happy, abundant, and ingenious expression" (xxv).

Yet Shakespeare's wholes are frequently defective. Although we are not given any examples of "defective" wholes, it is not difficult to see what Arnold is getting at: Shakespeare's plots rarely live up to Aristotle's (hence Arnold's) demand for "one entire and perfect action", witness his subplots and the many inconsistencies critics have pointed out in his dramas.

Another grievance, which is of course a consequence of Arnold's animosity against stylistic frills, is that sometimes it seems impossible for Shakespeare "to say a thing plainly" (xxvi). Arnold is proud to enlist "Mr. Hallam" as a brother in arms, who has had "the courage" to remark "how faultily difficult Shakespeare's language often is" (xxvi). And, as far as he himself is concerned, Arnold confesses that in some of the scenes of *King Lear* "every speech has to be read two or three times before it can be comprehended" (xxvii). Arnold tries to exonerate Shakespeare by means of a peculiar explanation: Shakespeare's linguistic exuberance can be accounted for by the fact that his audience was "far less cultivated and exacting" than the Athenian audience (xxvii).

The gist of Arnold's treatment of Shakespeare in the *Preface* is that he is good for the poetry reader, but not for the poetry writer. Arnold had no doubt that young poets should, figuratively speaking, be apprenticed to older and more experienced poets, preferably poets from another age than their own. Arnold did not want to deny Shakespeare's potential as a model (xxvii), but he regarded it as unfortunate if Shakespearean tendencies, where the details are valuable, but the composition of the whole is often worthless (xxv), were to find too many imitators. Actually, Keats' weaknesses are attributed by Arnold to the depraving influence of Shakespeare (xxv–xxvi).

Arnold's treatment of Shakespeare in the *Preface* is strangely biased. The latter's use of language and the absence of a moral message in his plays disqualifies him from meeting the requirements of *architectonicè*. It is remarkable that Shakespeare's metaphoric depth and richness of imagery should have left Arnold, a practising poet, cold. Therefore it is not a little puzzling to read Arnold's sonnet *Shakespeare*, which had been written in 1849, i.e. earlier than the *Preface*, and was included in the 1853 collection. The sonnet opens with the lines "Others

abide our question. Thou art free." That is a flat contradiction
to the lukewarm treatment awarded to Shakespeare in the
Preface, which left him anything but "free". The sonnet praises
Shakespeare for" out-topping knowledge", a point that was
barely hinted at in the *Preface*. When Arnold calls Shakespeare
"self-schooled, self-scanned, self-honoured, self-secure", he
echoes the formulation that Hamlet's father's ghost uses (I, 5,
77) when he describes the circumstances under which he was
"sent to my account": "unhouseled, disappointed, unaneled."
But, sadly enough, as we are told in the *Preface*, the wholes of
"that victorious brow" were deficient.

Form, Clough, Carlyle

Form

In his poetry, Arnold used a variety of forms: *Sohrab and
Rustum* is in blank verse, which Arnold may have found appro-
priate for a poem of "action". *Thyrsis* is in ten-line stanzas, and
the many sonnets that Arnold wrote obey the conventional
structures. In his narrative poems, Arnold frequently uses a
four-line stanza with four iambs in each line, and *The Strayed
Reveller* is in vers libre. Arnold confesses that when he began
writing *Thyrsis*, he was "carried irresistibly into this form", viz.
the model of Theocritus, "whom I have been much reading
during the two years this poem has been forming itself".[10]
Arnold's reflections on form are vitiated by the vagueness of
his terminology. In the *Preface*, he underlines the necessity for
a literary work to have a good "construction", "a consistently
drawn representation . . . not vaguely conceived and loosely
drawn" (xxviii), because "a representation which is general,
indeterminate and faint . . . does not add to our knowledge of
any kind" (xxviii). So the form ought to be harnessed to the
didactic purpose of the text. It is not enough for a poem to sat-
isfy a reader's "rhetorical sense", what should be gratified is his
"poetical sense" (xxiii). Neither of the senses is further devel-

oped, but we are allowed to conclude that 'rhetorical' refers to form. Arnold often returns to what he calls the "grand style", which he calls "excellent" (xxi), but which he does not analyse.

Another of Arnold's half-baked ideas is the suggestion that "boundaries and wholesome regulative laws" (xxx) would be helpful to poets. He calls for appropriate, but not too strict, rules that could serve as standards, and he reminds contemporary men of letters of their duty to be instrumental in establishing some guidelines. He ends the *Preface* on an exhortatory note: let us not give posterity the possibility of blaming us for neglecting the rules for good writing (xxx).

As Arnold sees it, there exists an almost God-given correspondence between the content of a given literary work and its form in the sense that the content determines the form. The form of a work" draws its force directly from the pregnancy of the matter it conveys" (xxi). If the appropriate form arises as an inevitable corollary of the subject, which seems to be bursting to get into the form it has itself chosen, Arnold's categorical statement "all depends upon the subject" becomes perfectly plausible. We may draw a parallel with many modern architects' byword "form follows function."

The danger was that too great formal sophistication might divert the reader's attention from the message of the text. That is the gist of Arnold's criticism of Shakespeare, who is blamed for his "over-curiousness of expression", which may sometimes jeopardize understanding (xxvii) Although Arnold hastens to add that "it is indeed but the excessive employment of a wonderful gift" (xxvii), he is still dissatisfied with Shakespeare's wholes.

In the Greek tragedies, Arnold saw a perfect subordination of form to content. The two work hand in glove: "the action itself, its selection and construction; this is what is all-important" (xxi), and the Greeks mastered the complete balance; they knew how to assign "the right degree of prominence" to what Arnold calls "expression" (xxi). To Arnold, the established and agreed form of the Greek tragedy had the indisputable advantage that it neither invited nor allowed much formal experimentation. In Sophocles and the other great trage-dians subject clearly took precedence over form. Virtually all their plays are cast in the same mould, and Arnold was fasci-nated by "the careful construction of the poem" (xxiii). That pleased his fondness for successful wholes. Arnold concedes that there may be a certain amount of "baldness" in the style of the Greeks, but that does not detract from its overall merits. The Greeks are "unapproached masters" in the handling of the balance (xxi). However, Arnold never gives an in-depth treat-ment of the structure of a classical Greek tragedy.

Clough

Arnold's general aloofness, in his literary criticism, from the technical aspects of form may seem the more remarkable in that Clough, who was his closest friend, and Carlyle, who was an acquaintance of his, found themselves at the centre of a heated debate over form among literati. In 1848, Clough had published *A Long-Vacational Pastoral* called *The Bothie of Tober-na-Vuolich*. It is a poem that describes the affection of Philip, a young Oxford radical, for Elspie, the daughter of a highland farmer. The setting and the subject were entirely palatable to Arnold, who later wrote several essays on the Celtic literary tradition and the correct way of appreciating it, but what triggered his serious concern was that Clough's poem was written in hexameters. Clough's choice of that unconventional metre was probably grounded on a wish to express a reaction against the hackneyed patterns used by the Romantic poets, i.e. a return to classicism that Arnold, who wrote extensively on Homer, might be expected to applaud.

   The Bothie fluttered the dovecotes and initiated some fierce polemics among critics, and Arnold was not alone in his insis-tence that the form of a literary work should under no circumstances be allowed to divert the reader's attention from the content. To Arnold, the problem was the more pressing in that his involvement in the contemporary Reform turmoil and the new religious ferment at Oxford made him feel the significance of content.

However, it was not only the hexameters of *The Bothie* that worried critics. An unsigned review from January 1849 in the *Spectator* of another of Clough's poems, *Ambarvalia* complains of "the careless obscurity, this throwing of fragments, as it were, to the reader as if he (sc. Clough) poured thoughts in verse without plan or purpose."[11] And John Conington reviews *Recent Poetry and Recent Verse* in *Frazer's Magazine* in May 1845 and blames Clough for "an obscurity of thought and a careless roughness of form."[12] Even if a poet "attempts small pictures," they should be "wholes and not *disjecta membra poetae.*"[13] Apparently there were some contemporaries who shared Arnold's predilection for *architectonicè*. The prevalent attitude was that of W.H. Smith, who wrote in *Dipsychus and the Letters of A.H. Clough* (*Macmillan's Magazine*, December 1866): "Do all we can . . . we are unable to reconcile ourselves to this verse, if verse it is to be called . . . the constant irritation of the (to us) detestable cadence would unfit us for any enjoyment at all."[14]

This prolonged debate and the inappropriateness of Clough's aberrations, as Arnold would call them, could not help but worry his friend Arnold, the more so as the two men saw eye to eye on many points. For example, they shared a great admiration for Goethe.

Carlyle

Carlyle was a towering figure in the intellectual debate of the better part of the 19th century, which Clough was not. In the words of Jules Seigel: "In a period marked by spiritual crises and the loss of religious faith by many Victorians, Carlyle's religious convictions and ethical pronouncements were taken very seriously."[15] Consequently, the heavyweights of the literary Parnassus of the former half of the 19th century engaged in discussions of Carlyle's views, and practically all of them have something to say about the way he performed linguistically.

In 1835, the critic John Sterling remarked on the strange style of *Sartor Resartus*: "A good deal of this is positively barbarous . . . the jerking, spasmodic, often violent syntax, and the use of inversion."[16] The statement is symptomatic, not only in its tone, but also in the fact that a critic of Carlyle goes into far greater detail with regard to syntax and choice of words than critics did with Clough's poems. Lady Sidney Morgan has this to say about the style of Carlyle's *French Revolution* (review in *Atheneum*, May 1837): "The book is full of quaintness and neologisms and a whimsical coxcombry," which she ascribes to German influence.[17] The idea of a possible German influence – which is not meant as a compliment – was taken up by John Stuart Mill, who reviews the *French Revolution* in *London's Westminster Review* in July 1837: "For a style more peculiar than that of Mr. Carlyle . . . does not exist . . . many sterling thoughts are so disguised in phraseology borrowed from the spiritualist school of German poets and metaphysicians as not only to obscure the meaning, but to raise, in the minds of most English readers, a not unnatural nor inexcusable presumption of there being no meaning at all."[18.] In a review article in *The Times* from August 1837, Thackeray fires a broadside at Carlyle's style: "Never did a man's style so mar his subject and dim his genius. It is stiff, short and rugged, it abounds with Germanisms and Latinisms, strange epithets and choking double words, astonishing to the admirers of simple Addisonian English . . . a man at the first onset must take breath at the end of a sentence, or, worse still, go to sleep in the midst of it."[19] Let us leave the last word to Edgar Allan Poe, who wrote extensively on Carlyle in the 1840s: "I would blame no man of sense for leaving the works of Carlyle unread . . . no man capable of producing a definite impression on his age or race, could or would commit himself to such inanities or insanities."[20]

The articles quoted above all date from a period before 1853, and Arnold may have known one or more of the contributors, but his voice is not heard in the ongoing heated debate about formal heterodoxy. What contemporary critics objected to was the sheer incomprehensibility of many of the novel approaches. John Sterling epitomizes the prevailing opinion (letter to Carlyle, May 1835): " . . . headlong, self-asserting capriciousness . . . is yet plainly to be seen in the structure of the sentences, the lawless oddity and the strange heterogeneous combinations and allusions . . . Among us, the subjective has risen into superiority and brought with it in each individual a multitude of peculiar associations and relations." Sterling proceeds to list a number of "suspicious words" and "compositions of words," "inversions which would not have been practised in conversation . . . accumulation and contrast of imagery."[21]

Between the lines, one can detect the longing that Arnold several times expressed for a regulatory body within the province of literature. Like many of his contemporaries he feared that stylistic fads might prove contagious or, even worse, become normative. However, the issue did not engage Arnold to such an extent that he was willing to commit himself to any effort in the hope of tipping the scales.

Concluding Remarks

In 1853, when Arnold wrote his *Preface*, there were no models and no accepted standards for such a composition. Interest in literature as literature was slender, so Arnold, who was only 31 in 1853, followed the example of earlier theorists like, for example, the Neo-Classicists (with whom he showed no great familiarity): he leant on criteria prescribed by revered predecessors, and his education and background made it natural for him to seek support in Aristotle and the works of the classical Greek dramatists, especially Sophocles.

The 1853 *Preface* is the presentation of a youthful Arnold's views on the task of poetry, the functions and duties of the poet and the critic, and the obligations of a potential poet. It is an elaboration of, and embroidering on, one central idea: the Greek tragedians are beyond any discussion the best, both in their own right and as models. The idea of somebody being able to serve as a model is of supreme significance for Arnold, at this early stage as well as in his later essays. Accordingly, their works should set the standard for all literature and be not only admired, but also imitated and emulated. The communication of this Neo-Classical and anti-contemporary message takes up the better part of the pages of the *Preface*. It is true that the *Preface* does touch upon other aspects of poetry, such as the contrast between Ancients and Moderns, *architectonicè*, and the necessity of having models, but they are derived from, and inextricably interwoven with, the Neo-Classical bias.

Arnold admired the "wholeness" of the classical tragedies, the felicitous blend of action and emotional restraint. Conveying the impression of totality ought to be the ultimate objective of a literary work (Arnold does not distinguish between genres), for that was a necessary precondition for it to be able to inculcate a moral. For the Aristotelian 'pity and fear', Arnold substitutes 'inspirit and rejoice'. However, the *summum bonum* may seem abstract, and we are left in the dark with regard to how it is to be achieved.

The *Preface* is, in some respects, a strange piece of writing in that the only poem that is referred to by name, viz. *Empedocles on Etna*, is the one that has not been included in the collection to which the *Preface* serves as an introduction. However, the argument for exclusion is an access road for Arnold to submit a poetical manifesto. The *Preface* is not a list of, or comment, on what a reader can expect to find in the collection. The prescriptions purportedly laid down for poetry in the *Preface* would be just as suitable for a tragedy, but Arnold's use of Aristotle's theories is selective. Thus, he leaves out the Stagirite's detailed reflections on form.

In a letter to Clough from October 10, 1853, Arnold states that "The *Preface* is done – there is a certain Geist in it, I think, but it is far less *precise* than I had intended. How difficult it is to write prose: and why? because of *the articulation of the discourse*; one leaps these over in poetry – places one thought cheek by jowl with another without introducing them and leaves them – but in prose this will not do; it is of course not right in poetry either – but we all do it."[22] The italics are Arnold's, and a modern reader is inclined to agree with him about the lack of precision, which is not only found in the vagueness of the terminology.

There is a good deal of self-assured rigidity and one-sidedness in the *Preface*: the ancients are unsurpassed, and it is impossible to write great poetry about Arnold's own time. The *Preface* is a controversial piece of writing containing a good many idiosyncratic postulates. However, Arnold does not want to open a debate but to hammer home a message. It is true that he endeavours to be scrupulously fair to opponents and sceptics, witness his tip-toe approach in the benign assessment of Shakespeare, still some of the pages of the *Preface* read like the words of a man preaching a sermon.

The *Preface* is not a solid rocky ground on which Arnold came to build a theoretical superstructure. Many of the views that appear in the *Preface* are played down or do not occur in Arnold's later critical oeuvre. Thus, 'action', which is a keystone of the *Preface* virtually disappears in the later literary essays. On the other hand, some of the ideas that are central to Arnold's later criticism, for example that content should take precedence over form, are made manifest as early as in the *Preface*.

Altogether, the *Preface* which, as evidenced by the letters to Clough, is the fruit of years of reflection, is recognizably Arnold's work: the purpose of a text should be to edify its reader, for which reason it ought to exemplify the best that is said and thought. Arnold never questioned the duty and the power of literature to edify mankind, and he never tired of hammering home his doctrines. Sometimes – also in his later essays – he reads like a propagandist rather than a literary or a social critic.

His criteria of acceptance widened as he grew older, but they never fundamentally altered or transgressed his overall framework. Arnold never became a literary historian or a motif-hunter.

CHAPTER FOUR

INFLUENCES: GOETHE AND SAINTE-BEUVE

"No man is an Iland, intire in itselfe." That often quoted statement by John Donne[1] applies also to an author. Some authors claim to receive their inspiration by divine grace; others borrow (or steal!) from their contemporaries and predecessors. The common designation for the phenomenon is influence.

Influence may derive from several sources. From early in his life, Arnold immersed himself in a cult of the Classics. His father, the headmaster, had a profound interest in, and expert knowledge of, Greek historians, as exemplified by Thucydides.[2] Also Goethe, whom Arnold referred to as "the greatest critic of our age", could lay claim to being a classical scholar, and since Goethe and Sainte-Beuve are the most frequently quoted critics in Arnold's literary essays, it is permissible to conclude that they were sources of inspiration.

Arnold never openly acknowledged any indebtedness to either Goethe or Sainte-Beuve – or to any other critic. In most cases, he limits himself to laudatory one-sentence pats on the shoulder, amounting to little more than names-dropping. Yet the references to Goethe and Sainte-Beuve are different in that they are more frequent, and perceptive enough to prove that Arnold knew them and was familiar with their ideas.

Goethe

The differences between Arnold and Goethe as critics and men of letters leap to the eye. For one thing, Goethe was a profounder and far more versatile intellect than Arnold. Unlike Arnold, Goethe did not turn his back on non-humanistic pursuits: he was an expert on optics, he had more than a nodding acquaintance with mineralogy and botany, he was a competent connoisseur of music and the visual arts, he was a practising painter, and he wrote a book on the theory of colours (*Farbenlehre*).

Also, as far as literature was concerned, his scope was far wider than Arnold's: he displayed great insight into the theory and practice of the drama,[3] he translated Voltaire and Diderot, and he was an admiring reader of English novels. Eckermann describes how, in 1837, Goethe gave an analysis of Sir Walter Scott's *Rob Roy* and Dr Johnson's *Rasselas*.[4]

Most importantly in the context of these pages, the German poet had no distinct 'message' to convey, and the attitude to Shakespeare demonstrates the difference between the two men. Goethe admits that Shakespeare did not follow the Aristotelian principles, but claimed that he was a genius who could only be appreciated against the backdrop of his own age and the prevalent national tradition. Varenne notices[5] that, in 1824, Goethe expressed great admiration of Shakespeare's knowledge of human character, and, more generally, of the technical skill of the Elizabethan dramatists. Goethe says nothing at all about Shakespeare's potential as a moral exemplum.

Goethe frequently mentions his intimacy with literature. In 1824, Eckermann quotes him for saying that "Mein eigentliches Glück war mein poetisches Sinnen und Schaffen."[6] Arnold would probably not disagree but was somehow too shy to give such an open confession. Goethe told Eckermann that it is incumbent on poets not just to record historic events, but to offer something higher and better. Look to the Greeks: they were less concerned with historic facts than with the possibilities of a poetical treatment of them[7]. Such treatment warranted the need for action, Arnold would suggest. In 1831, Goethe said that perfect poetry demanded the Truly Great and Pure; it invites the readers to strive upwards towards the "other nature". The words read like a page out of Arnold.

The two men see eye to eye on the detrimental effects of defective poetry. Neither of them attempts anything like a definition of such poetry, or of its opposite. But they have no doubt that it is harmful to its readers because they would absorb the poet's failings.[8] On the contrary, a great dramatist whose noble soul penetrates all his plays will be able to obtain a pervasive dissemination of that noble soul among his readers. The thought is echoed in the last pages of Arnold's *Preface*. Goethe exemplifies his postulate by asserting that the tragedies of Corneille contributed to developing contemporary conceptions of the hero.

That is why antiquity is at the forefront of both Goethe's and Arnold's attention. In 1827, Goethe maintained that the study of the writers of antiquity may be instrumental in shaping a reader's character, especially, of course, if the latter is the kind of human being in whom God has planted the talent of recognizing spiritual greatness.[9] Arnold's almost identical version of that opinion occurs towards the end of the *Preface*. Goethe is satisfied that the ancients were objective in the sense that they strove to give a truthful picture of the world. The Romantic poets' subjectivity, however, was a blind alley, he said in 1826.[10] We can almost hear Arnold's applause.

The treatment of Byron is symptomatic. Goethe said in the opening pages of his essay on Byron, "Aber Byron ist nur gross wenn er dichtet. Sobald er reflektiert, ist er ein Kind."[11] In the first pages of his essay on Byron, Arnold states that the latter's reflections are those of a child. The essay proceeds to pay tribute to Byron as a rhetorician, and Arnold's final verdict is an almost verbatim translation of Goethe: Byron was a fine poet, but a miserable philosopher.[12]

There are several seemingly half-digested and strangely incomplete pronouncements in Arnold's *Preface*. Thus, Arnold states that criticism is a prerequisite for poetic creativity. The idea is not elaborated and remains cryptic (xxvi). However, a glance at some of Goethe's statements as quoted by Eckermann helps to shed some light on the mystery. As Goethe saw it, poetic inspiration arose on the basis of a poet's preoccupation with the works of critics. Thus, Goethe himself claimed to have received the ideas for some of his works from his reading of various critical studies on Homer. Those studies taught him that, like criticism, poetry is more than the observation of rules.[13]

Arnold was convinced that rational argumentation and "seeing things as they are" (the implication always being "and not as scientists claim they are") had huge persuasive and restorative powers. Even if he would later divide his fellow countrymen into three categories, viz. Populace, Philistines, and Barbarians, his view of the beneficial impact of literature was not class-bound: everybody was called upon to familiarize themselves with "the best that is said and thought" and to discover their "best self" by disinterestedly "looking into themselves". It is clearly implied that everybody, irrespective of class affiliation, has a potential "best self" worth exploring, and that salvation is not a privilege of a minority.

On that point, too, Goethe and Arnold are kindred spirits. Goethe several times returns to the poet's obligation never to lose sight of 'das Gemeine', i.e. that which is common to all mankind. Goethe wished that spiritual awakening and higher education might become 'ein Gemeingut', i.e. a benefit shared by the many.[14] More than once Goethe criticizes his contemporaries for remaining stuck in mediocrity, and consequently disregarding what is Really Great. The poet, he said in 1825,[15] should seize 'das Besondere', i.e. the specific, and, if it is healthy, he should strive to elevate it into 'das Gemeine', i.e. the general. The idea of 'the general' as the superstructure and sophistication of 'the specific' was grist to Arnold's mill. Actually he quoted the two German terms in their original language several times.

Much of what Goethe wrote is didactic: *The Elective Affinities* discusses the relationship between natural law and moral law, and *Wilhelm Meister's Lehrjahre* deals, among other things, with the problem of renunciation. However, unlike Arnold, Goethe had some misgivings with regard to the purpose of literature. For example, in 1866, he expressed some concern for the artist's creative liberty and development if didacticism is to be the sole purpose.[16] That problem is non-existent for Arnold.

Even if Goethe did not create any original or groundbreaking critical concepts, his approach is not only far more purely literary, but also more wide-ranging that Arnold's. Goethe's value judgements are based on far more solid ground than those of Arnold, who comes to appear not only as a tight-lipped aunt, but also as a man of far lesser stature that the German giant.

Goethe was the author who had the single greatest impact on Arnold as a man of letters. Arnold never goes into any detail about his indebtedness – he just took what he felt he needed, and the *Geistesverwandschaft* is perceptible from Arnold's formative years and onwards. That applies sometimes to the very formulation of the ideas. No doubt, many of the fundamental views shared by the two men were current topics in the age in which they lived, but the relevant thing is that Arnold frequently – explicitly or implicitly – turned to the Continent for inspiration or confirmation.

Sainte-Beuve

Literary portraits were not unknown in French literature by the time Sainte-Beuve began to write. The *Caractères* (1694) of Jean de la Bruyère (1645–96) are a series of observations on conduct, moralizing in content and pessimistic in tone. La Bruyère passed judgement, and poured scorn, on the vanities of the men and the frivolities of the women he saw around him.

The approach of Charles-Auguste de Sainte-Beuve

(1804–69) was psychological rather than moralizing. His *Portraits littéraires* (1836–39), *Causeries du Lundi* (1851–62) and *Nouveaux Lundis* (1863–69) earned him the surname "the father of modern criticism" because he was responsible for the transformation of literary criticism from a minor to a major form of art.

One of his tenets, and one which influenced Arnold considerably, was that the critic should provide data for the formative influences on an author's character, for example psychological inheritance, social background, education, love, friendship, etc. Such information would lead to a better understanding of a writer's artistic creation, indeed, would form the necessary basis for it to be possible to give a truthful verdict on the work. It will be seen that such background is a storehouse of objective facts, i.e. something that can be counted and measured, and accordingly in line with Positivist philosophy. Sainte-Beuve claimed himself that his intention with his critical work was to supply criticism with some *"charme, réalité, poésie et psychologie."*[17]

Sainte-Beuve's essay on Corneille (1828) may serve as an exemplar of his technique. The text opens with some theoretical reflections on the particular kind of pleasure that can be derived from reading the French tragedians. The critic's task, we are told, is to examine the general condition of literature at a time when a new author makes his appearance. The necessity of giving biographical data about the writer being analysed is stressed. Next follows a meticulous description of Corneille's oeuvre, accompanied by evaluations. The style and characteristics of his plays are commented on, and at the end Sainte-Beuve sums up with a general characterization of *"un genie sûr"*, who sometimes reached the stars, but who, admittedly, at others moved closer to the ground.

Beyond any doubt, Sainte-Beuve was the critic who, with his biographical method, provided Arnold with a mould in which to couch his literary reflections. Arnold's essay on Heine is a case in point: beginning with an excursus on the tasks of a critic, the essay goes on to account for Goethe's influence on Heine. Next follow some fairly detailed biographical facts, and the essay is rounded off with an empathetic characterization of the German poet and his work.

The structural ingredients and the progression found in Sainte-Beuve's *portraits* are recognizable in many of Arnold's essays, not only those dealing with literary figures. By the same token, it seems unlikely that Arnold would, unassisted, have come across the name of the young French poet Maurice de Guérin. He was the subject of a long essay by Sainte-Beuve, but he was virtually unknown in England. Incidentally, preoccupation with Guérin prompted Arnold to write probably his most thorough-going pages of literary criticism.

However, sometimes Sainte-Beuve's method would go into overdrive. In his essay about Racine, Sainte-Beuve enumerates a number of biographical data on the basis of which he draws some conclusions about the French dramatist's character and habits. In turn, those inferences form the launch pad for more far-reaching conclusions which are, in some cases, pure conjecture.

CHAPTER FIVE

THE SCHOOLS INSPECTOR AND ESSAY WRITER

Matthew Arnold combined the job of an inspector of schools with the activity of a prolific writer of essays and review articles. In 1859 and 1865, he was sent on official business to study educational systems on the Continent. The fruits of his journeys, *The Popular Education of France* (1861) and *Schools and Universities on the Continent* (1868) drew attention to English deficiencies in educational matters, especially as far as secondary education was concerned. The two books are symptomatic of Arnold's general approach to the subjects he tackles: broad outlines, well-intentioned suggestions, few genuine in-depth reflections on what he saw in the fields of learning and teaching. Pedagogic ideas, curriculum issues, and the role and tasks of the teacher are given scant attention. Yet some of his suggestions actually led to various educational initiatives in contemporary England. There are vague references to educational issues in both *Culture and Anarchy* and *Friendship's Garland*, and the schoolmasterly tone is recognizable in most of what Arnold wrote, but in the light of his life-long work within the schools system, the extent to which such subjects are kept at arm's length is remarkable.

Arnold's evaluative criteria were based on idiosyncratic morality rather than empirical evidence. Hence his essays sometimes read like the disappointed realization of an impatient schoolmaster taking a slow pupil to task. The raised forefinger is not difficult to identify, the schoolmaster's responsibility is constantly taken into account. Interestingly, in his literary essays Arnold also behaves as a teacher, eg, when he wants to instruct fledgling poets in the art of writing a successful poem.

The Essays

Arnold published numerous collections of essays: *Essays in Criticism* (1865 & 1888), *Mixed Essays* (1870), *Irish Essays* (1882), but he had also review articles printed in periodicals and newspapers, e.g. *Spinoza*, published in *The London Review* in 1862 on the occasion of the first English translation of the Dutch philosopher's *Tractatus Theologico-Politicus* from 1670.

The essays, appearing over a thirty-year period – the *Shakespeare* essay is from 1853 and *Literature and Science* from 1882 – cover a wide range of subjects: religion (*Athens and Israel* [1878]), philosophy (*Marcus Aurelius* [1863]), and social and political affairs (*Culture and Anarchy* [1869]). A large number of the essays are devoted to literature, theoretical pieces (*The Function of Criticism at the Present Time* [circa 1864]) and monographs (*Chaucer* [1880]). The latter comprise a few classical authors (*On Translating Homer* [1861]), but the main emphasis is on authors that are closer to Arnold's own age, especially the English Romantic poets.

Unlike the two authors who were his most important mentors, viz. Goethe and Sainte-Beuve, Arnold was not interested in either the visual arts or music. Hardly any composer's name or work crops up in the essays, and if a painter or sculptor is mentioned, the latter only appears as a necessary supplement in a context, and not for any intrinsic interest the artist may possess.

More generally, a modern reader may find it a weakness that Arnold gives very few examples or references to concrete works. In his essays about the Romantic poets, for example, he takes it for granted that the reader will be so familiar with the depicted author's oeuvre that a mere word or an ultra-brief quotation will suffice for the reader to set the whole paragraph, or even article, into perspective. The examples Arnold does furnish in many cases read like names-dropping, and not infrequently they confer an air of hasty work, or even superficiality, on his presentation.

Science

Even if few of Arnold's essays have science as their main subject or include the word science in their titles – an exception being *Literature and Science*, written in 1882 and published in 1885 – the rapidly advancing scientific paradigm filled Arnold with grave misgivings. In practically all his essays, also the non-literary ones, Arnold distances himself, implicitly or explicitly, from the doctrines and line of thought of contemporary scientists. He does not have an eye for the many practical inventions that were fruits of scientific progress, and which made science so popular with many ordinary people. To Arnold, science was synonymous with crass materialism and the disappearance of God. But it was a formidable adversary because it was instrumental in constructing a social model.

Arnold objected to scientists' definition of truth: they acknowledged as truth only what was demonstrable and provable, i.e. what could be measured, counted, and weighed. They were able to show how the "natural laws" that they had established by means of a mixture of induction and deduction provided a picture of 'reality' that was incontrovertible and of universal validity. That explanation of reality came to seem so obvious that alternatives had to fight an uphill struggle. And here, Arnold was a kind of piggy in the middle: on the one hand he realized that he would have to undertake the job of uneasy adaptation to the scientific pattern if he was to gain a hearing and obtain recognition of his ideas. Thus, his demand for 'disinterestedness' in criticism has a striking similarity with the scientific demand for objectivity. But on the other hand his philosophy was only demonstrable with reference to his personal experience and conviction, which could never obtain parity of esteem with a mathematical theorem, and which could not be confirmed by 'natural laws', let alone claim universal validity. What Arnold fought for was the establishment of criteria for the truth of literary works against the onslaught of a system of examining, testing, and proving that had taunted literary works with the predicate of being "mere invention", a blind alley that yielded no results that could be documented, hence, ultimately, a waste of time.

Perceptibly ill at ease, Arnold had to operate within the scientific paradigm in his pursuit of truth and verification, but all he felt able to suggest in the way of verification was "to let reason and the will of God prevail", to "allow the free play of the mind" on "the best that is known and thought in the world."

Mid-19th century science patented concepts like truth and reality. Only towards the end of the century were physicists and mathematicians grudgingly forced to acknowledge that their field of study did not provide an exhaustive explanation, and that 'reality' comprises a plethora of intangible ingredients like illusions, dreams, and myths, not to speak of religion and philosophy. Especially in the latter half of the 19th century, the humanities began to respond to science's pretensions by acknowledging science's results, but at the same time insisting that there are areas where the scientific approach is insufficient and inapplicable, for example in ethics and many aspects of art.

Like many of his contemporaries, Arnold feared science's elimination of God and, more generally, of spiritual values. To Stuart Mill, for example, science was an enemy to man. That attitude slowly gained ground during the last decades of the 19th century, and with the advent of the Imagists after the turn of the century, the Positivist concept of reality was toppled, and a radical redefinition of the concept of reality was propounded.[1]

Arnold also disliked, and was suspicious of, the method of science: starting on the basis of a series of individual observations and proceeding stepwise to establish a totality was diametrically opposed to Arnold's procedure. He persistently stressed the necessity of beginning with "an idea of the world", a philosophy of life, and viewing discrete phenomena in the light of that perfect ideal. "The idea is everything, the rest is a world of illusion," he wrote in *The Study of Poetry*.[2] Poetry is a moral provided with linguistic trimmings. We may note in passing that Arnold's revered master, Sainte-Beuve did not start his essays with a preconceived theory as a guiding principle for what literature ought to be and do. And Arnold never gave the shadow of a rational explanation of such overriding ideas that would go down with the Positivists. They were satisfied that *they* had got hold of "the best that is said and thought".

Arnold's top-to-bottom approach was caused by his fear of being knocked over by what he called 'the multitudinousness' of the world, and 'multitudinousness' was science's field of operation. One of his grievances against poets like Shelley and Keats was the very fact that their incessant efforts to find the pithy and striking image and the melodious flow of the lines led to a blurring of the totality, the 'idea' of many of their poems. Arnold acknowledged Keats' greatness as a poet (he was less comfortable with Shelley), but on several occasions he said that the Romantic poets "did not know enough". The reason was probably that, having no overall 'idea', they never got beyond what Arnold considered superficial mellifluousness, they could not see the wood for the trees. Like the scientists, the Romantic poets tended to use a bottom-to-top approach, the difference being, as Arnold saw it, that they never achieved what really mattered – *architectonicè*.

In Arnold's essays, we witness a life-long struggle to get to grips with the Beast in Revelations. Few of his essays deliver a full-scale attack on science, but in Arnold's allusions and innuendoes the reader detects an undertone of uneasiness and scepticism, but also of stubborn defiance. For example, in *St. Paul and Protestantism* Arnold attempts a definition of God as a being where "the religious and the scientific sense may meet."[3]

In *On the Study of Celtic Literature*, he tries to "tame" science by making it a humanistic discipline, at the same time insisting that, as the elder sister, poetry can lay claim to at least parity of esteem. The idea is pursued in *Culture and Anarchy*, which looks upon science and the arts as two sides of the concept of culture. The late essay *Literature and Science* (1882) – one of the few articles that includes science in its title – raises the question how the achievements of "humane letters" are compatible with the results of science.[4] Arnold has no doubt that "humane letters" are a necessary component "in a man's training." A glance at the past, he says, will show that "poetry and eloquence" have "a fortifying, and elevating, and quickening, and suggestive power" (an echo of a passage in the 1853 *Preface*), which pulls well with the fruits of science, which are, of course, to be "frankly accepted." Arnold staunchly defends the position, "now and in the future", of "humane letters" as represented, for example, by Greek culture, and he expresses the hope that the success story of science can somehow be related to man's innate need for "conduct" and beauty.

The essay reads like an incantation and a cry of distress: by the 1880s, science had reached the apex of its predominance, and Arnold, the classically trained scholar, was feeling beleaguered.

Eliot

Incidentally, Arnold's idiosyncratic use of scientific terminology in his non-scientific philosophy may have been at the root of T.S. Eliot's life-long mixture of reluctant respect and downright scorn where Arnold was concerned.

In his book, *Matthew Arnold and the Betrayal of Language*,[5] David Riede makes an interesting point: Arnold found himself in a linguistic dilemma because the current theoretical language was characterized by scientific precision and seemed eminently appropriate for the description of an objective world,[6] but not for a definition of "the best that is thought and said". Arnold acknowledged that science expands our knowledge, but insisted that its terminology is incapable of doing justice to "human experience and aspiration." However, value judgements are not recognized by scientific terminology, so all Arnold could do was to quote examples from literary works and to appeal to "critical tact" and refer to "what experience shows."[7] But still he claimed truth value and reliable verification for his postulates. To the Positivists, truth was accordance with demonstrable and demonstrated factors in 'reality' i.e. the world outside man. To Arnold, truth was an inner conviction, a question of subjective, hence unprovable, belief. To the Positivists, verification was the result of a process of presumed objective rational inductions and deductions. To Arnold, it was an intuitive realization.

The American philosopher Francis Herbert Bradley (1846–1924) was Eliot's philosophy teacher at Harvard, and Eliot wrote an unpublished doctoral dissertation on him. His teaching and his doctrines about "immediate sense impressions" made a profound impression on Eliot, who refers to him again and again with unstinting and respectful praise.[8]

Arnold seems to have been one of Bradley's pet aversions for the very reason that Arnold's vocabulary encroached on scientific terminology. "What does 'verify' actually mean?" he asked with reference to Arnold's invocation of scientific blessing for his use of the word. Such dubious substantiation provoked Bradley, and consequently also Eliot. Eliot was not enthusiastic about the Positivist world picture, but he was under the sway of his Harvard teacher, and took over a good deal of Bradley's scepticism. He developed a love/hate relationship to Arnold. References to Arnold crop up in many of Eliot's works, also in non-Arnoldian contexts. Eliot was obviously so fascinated by Arnold the man and his philosophy that he had to return to him again and again. But he never really seems to have made up his mind about Arnold. His attitude alternates between respect for Arnold's overall achievement ("he is in some respects the most

satisfactory man of letters of his age"[9]) and patronizing head-shaking ("In philosophy and theology he was an undergraduate"[10]), thus turning Arnold's blame of the Romantic poets against himself.

However, Eliot definitely has a point when he says that Arnold "placed an exaggerated emphasis on morals",[11] and still in the same essay (*The Use of Poetry and the Use of Criticism*), he makes the following idiosyncratic observation: "And when we know his poetry, we are not surprised that in his criticism he tells us little or nothing about his experience of writing it, and that he is so little concerned with poetry from the maker's point of view."[12]

Eliot had an eye for Arnold's neglect of a more theoretical approach to poetry, which he attributes to superficiality and a lack of understanding on Arnold's part. One of Arnold's pronouncements that provoked a particularly scornful reaction on Eliot's part was that "poetry is a criticism of life." However, here it is relevant to point out two things: first Eliot perpetrates a piece of disingenuousness by dislodging the statement from its context. In its entirety, it runs as follows: "Poetry is a criticism of life. It should follow the laws of its own nature and keep free of the practical view of things,"[13] which not only deprives Eliot's jibe of some of its sting, but also comes very close to Eliot's own conception of poetry. And in *Literature and Science* from 1862, Arnold says that "Poetry and eloquence are the criticism of life by gifted men alive and active with extraordinary power at an unusual number of points",[14] which may seem evident, but is at least inoffensive.

Secondly, Eliot seems to ignore, or forget, that Arnold's criticism is never exclusively literary. It is part and parcel of the philosophical, religious, social and political edifice he attempts to erect, and that is what justifies his maxim that "poetry is a criticism of life." To Eliot, literature was a thing in its own right, an ethereal phenomenon that must not be sullied by earth-bound trammels. To Arnold, who rarely used the word literature, a text was a tool to help readers in their struggle upwards towards moral perfection.

ARNOLD AS A LITERARY CRITIC

The Function of Criticism at the Present Time

The essay *The Function of Criticism at the Present Time* (circa 1864[1]) gives a good picture of Arnold as a literary critic. Even though the word 'literary' does not appear in the title, Arnold says himself that his business in the essay is with literature, and the essay contains useful reflections on poetry and criticism. The essay is symptomatic of Arnold's approach, in terms of content as well as "construction".

The Function of Criticism at the Present Time is a ramble through heterogeneous matter: there is a tribute to Edmund Burke for his rejection of the French Revolution, a vague comment on the contrast concentration/expansion, a pious hope that the current "passionate" material progress will eventually lead to a spiritual uplift – "it seems to be indispensable;" hortatory advice to farmers and tradesmen, followed by a praise of the old Anglo-Saxon race. Next, there is a comment on the recent murder of a child and the subsequent reaction of the press, which provokes the final fanfare, "we are not the best."

The essay is a mixture of idiosyncratic postulates, obstinate value judgements, and seemingly unmotivated abrupt shifts from one subject to another. In those respects, the essay is a characteristic specimen of Arnold's usual procedure. However, in the essay Arnold also to some extent lifts the veil of discretion surrounding his views on poetry and criticism.

Terminological Vagueness

The task of criticism is to exercise curiosity "to try to know the best that is said and thought in the world."[2] The material of literature is "the best ideas on every matter which is touches, current at the time."[3] The interesting point here, viz. that literature should take its starting-point in ideas, is partly undermined by the fact that, neither here nor elsewhere – and the formulation "best ideas" occurs frequently in his oeuvre – does Arnold give the barest hint of what such ideas may be, or who found out that they actually *were* the best.

Most of his observations on literature in this essay are equally applicable to poetry and prose, and, as we saw above, the pattern of the 1853 *Preface* bears more than a faint resemblance to a theory of the drama. By the same token, much of what Arnold says about poetry in *The Function* . . . might, without major changes, be said about criticism, which is no wonder considering the intimate kinship Arnold saw between poetry and criticism. But sometimes the lumping together of the two leads to fogginess and contradictions, for example when it comes to a discussion of the role to be played by novelty and tradition respectively.

Arnold pays tribute to creativity, which seems to be a processing of "the best that is said and thought", i.e. tradition.[4] Yet, a few pages further on we read that a poet should be able to draw on a reservoir of fresh thought,[5] and that criticism should not go with the stream.[6] The meaning could be that the creative element is not the finding of something quite new, but the leaning on the part of the existing body of ideas that are agreed to be the best. Judgment (Arnold's spelling) and application are deemed insufficient by Arnold for the very reason that they do not involve creativity.

Poetical creation is the offspring of ideas. A poet is admonished to read books that will enable him to "construct a semblance of the world in his own mind."[7] A poet should familiarize himself with the world he lives in, and with the life people actually live, before he starts to deal with them in his work, but then again, his approach must not be too "practical," because "the practical man" sees life from too narrow an angle.[8]

What inspired Arnold to write *The Function . . .* was, by his own admission, the deplorable plight of contemporary criticism – not only literary criticism. If we keep Arnold's theory about the dependence of literary creation on criticism in mind, we understand that, in his view, the weak position of the latter would inevitably depreciate the power and the value of English literature. In Arnold's idiolect, the basis of criticism is the existing body of written ideas on philosophical, theological, social, and literary subjects and attitudes. "Poetry requires a great critical effort behind it."[9] However, Arnold is not blind to the part played by the poet. "The creative power is outside the poet's control."[10] Somehow, creation seems also to include the particular findings of a gifted individual who follows the law of its (sc. criticism's) own nature, which is "a free play of the mind on all subjects which is touches."[11] If that law is not obeyed, "a nation's spirit dies of inanition."[12] That is where Arnold saw a real danger, for the English are not fond of abstract thinking, and generally, they tend to despise ideas.

Arnold deplores the absence, in English criticism, of a "mental dimension" that would contribute to leading mankind away from the prevalent smugness, instead enabling it to dwell on "the beauty and fitness of things."[13] What he somewhat obscurely calls 'judgment' (his spelling) is not enough for the very reason that it does not involve creativity. In several passages of his oeuvre, Arnold intimates that it would be a blessing for English intellectual life to have an institution reminiscent of, but not identical with, the French academy. Such a body could lay down the rules for correct and successful writing. However, Arnold never shows any real engagement in the subject; it is as if the idea at the same time fascinates him and scares him, so he drops it. The whole issue is another instance of a potentially fertile discussion being left at the roadside by Arnold.

"Criticism should ask itself how it can be useful."[14] Eliot asked the same question in the book whose title may have been inspired by the Arnoldean formulation (*The Use of Poetry and the Use of Criticism*). Neither of them ventured a suggestion about how and to whom their idiosyncratic concept of criticism might be useful. Both of them maintain that criticism should be on a higher level than earth-bound matter-of-factness and evaluation of individual phenomena. That is as far as we get. To Arnold, one of the criteria for good criticism is "disinterestedness".

In *The Function . . .* , there are envious references to the standard of criticism in Germany and France. Arnold was very inspired by Goethe's criticism; on the surface we remain on the ultra-brief value judgement stage; however, as demonstrated earlier in this book,[15] Goethe's thinking permeates many of the views Arnold expresses in his essays, sometimes down to the very formulation.

On the last page of *The Function . . .* , Arnold sums up his demand on criticism: it should be creative and sincere, simple, flexible, ardent, ever widening its knowledge. It should be the opposite of a poor, starved, fragmentary, inadequate creation.[16] As was his habit, Arnold does not exemplify his criteria with the name of an author or a work.

The sum total of all this is a heap of confusion, not least because conflicting statements are expressed with equal conviction at a few pages' distance from each other. Whether Arnold did not see the inconsistency, or whether it was due to hasty writing or sloppy thinking, remains unexplained. At any rate, Arnold made no attempt to balance them, and once more he raises more hares than he brings down.

Maurice de Guérin

The Man and His Poetry

The French Romantic poet Maurice de Guérin (1810–39) was in several important respects a man to Arnold's liking. It is possible that, with his knowledge of French literature, Arnold "discovered" him for himself. Still, it seems likely that he got some inspiration from the essay that Sainte-Beuve wrote about him.

Guérin was religious, but attracted by a kind of pagan pantheism. In his slightly mystical poetry he sought inspiration in the kind of Hellenism that fascinated Arnold. Guérin confessed himself that he was possessed of a "most bizarre imagination,"[17] but he was no great literary theorist. As a matter of fact, his letters are generally of little interest. Many of them are addressed to his sister Eugénie, who seems to have been a kindred spirit and to whom he speaks openly about his thoughts, his ever worsening disease (tuberculosis), and his permanent difficulties in having his writings published.

However, there are one or two stray remarks that may have caught Arnold's attention: in a letter from 1829, Guérin deplores the Romantic poets' lack of vision; what poetry needs is energy and constancy,[18] and in a later letter (from 1836) he brushes aside the issue of form and opines that a poet should submit to "the sensible laws of the imagination."[19]

Arnold's Essay

Arnold's essay on Maurice de Guérin, which dates from 1862–3,[20] is more interesting for what it says about the writing of poetry than about the French poet. Actually, it is one of Arnold's most informative pieces of theoretical writing. It is a paradox that Arnold, who generally despised the Romanticists, should be so enthusiastic about, and inspired by, one of the representatives of the category – albeit a foreigner.

On the first page, Arnold extols the "interpretative power of poetry . . . the power of so dealing with things as to awaken in us a wonderfully full, new, and intimate sense of them, and of our relations with them."[21] As could be expected, Arnold makes in passing one of his derogatory allusions to science, which appeals to a much more "limited faculty": Shakespeare is better than Linnaeus to give us "the true sense of animals, or water, or plants."[22]

What singles out Guérin, Arnold suggests, is his outstanding capacity to illustrate "this magical power of poetry" – especially in his prose, which is only a seeming paradox, for here Arnold obviously uses 'poetry' in the sense of 'literature'. To Guérin, poetry interprets the world of nature as well as the world of morals. Such words were sweet music to Arnold's ears.

For a brief moment, Arnold ventures tentatively into the realm of form: Guérin has "the most profound and delicate sense of the life of nature, and the most exquisite felicity in finding expression to render that sense."[23] Arnold again voices his suspicion of some metres of poetry (now we are back in the category of poems): the alexandrine and the heroic couplet are often deplorably inadequate, whereas blank verse may occasionally pass muster.[24]

In Guérin's perception, 'Nature' comprises not only the world that surrounds us, but also "the life of man."[25] Arnold could not agree more: what is conventionally known as "nature poetry" should also contain "wholesome thoughts." So, the road is open for another of Arnold's by now familiar lashes at the Romantic poets: "that youthful literature which has put forth all its blossoms prematurely." Even the best known ones among them did not manifest "one of those sweet and wholesome thoughts which nourish the human soul."[26]

What makes the above passages particularly significant and slightly intriguing is that they so explicitly expose Arnold's dilemma in regard to the Romantic poets. For after disapproving of their intellectual superficiality, Arnold proceeds to celebrate their natural magic.[27]

As far as nature poetry in the sense of what the Greeks called *physis* is concerned, Guérin seems to be an unsurpassed master and, accordingly he serves as the standard of comparison. To him, as well as to Keats, nature was *magna mater*. Keats' and Guérin's "temperament" has given to the fruits of their genius a unique brilliancy and flavour,[28] and in *Ode to Autumn* Keats has actually "rendered nature", whereas Shelley, whose talent was predominantly musical, has unsuccessfully *tried* to render it in *Lines written in the Euganean Hills.* Arnold states that, in general, Shelley does not obtain "the natural magic" in his poems.[29]

"Natural magic," however, is only one half of perfection. Arnold is a staunch defender of the maxim that really great poets combine the naturalistic and the moralistic although he willingly admits that in some poets – Wordsworth is a case in point – the moral may be made too explicit.

Arnold's essay ends, rather anti-climactically, with a page-long quotation from Guérin's *The Centaur.* It is hard to see how such *Sturm und Drang* verbiage can have fascinated Arnold. That quotation may be typical of the level of Guérin's general poetic achievement, for the rest of the poem is no better. Therefore, it seems beyond doubt that Arnold exaggerates Guérin's stature. He read into the Frenchman's life and works "a search for perfection"[30], which may be what he fell for. With Guérin, Arnold created an idealized figure whom he could use as a touchstone for, and confirmation of, some of his own theories.

As is usual with Arnold, this essay uses postulates rather than arguments; yet the passages dealing with the Romantic poets are more *nuancés* than Arnold's numerous other references to them. And it is refreshing to see Arnold for once don the gown of the *literary* critic.

Concluding Remarks

For all his insistence on 'disinterestedness', Arnold's literary criticism was heavily biased, and for all his emphasis on wholeness, it was selective and fragmentary, not only in relation to the treatment of individual authors, but also in terms of a more comprehensive overview.

In Arnold's critical interest, there is a huge vacuum between Homer and the Greek tragedians, and Goethe. It is true that some attention is given to Shakespeare. However, he receives a schoolmasterly reprimand for his moral deficiency rather than being evaluated as a dramatist. One of the key words of the 1853 *Preface* is 'action'. However, the multifarious types of action staged by the Elizabethan dramatists did not appeal to Arnold. The intellectual climate of the French Enlightenment with its social, political, and literary pioneering efforts is passed over in silence. Men like Voltaire and Diderot showed some of the uses to which literature could be put, but at the same time they were virulently anticlerical, which may account for Arnold's complete disregard of them. With his *Lives of the Poets*, Dr Johnson had blazed a trail that Arnold was to follow, but the Great Lexicographer, as well as other important 18th century figures found no favour with Arnold – a possible exception being Gray.

Arnold wrote extensively on the Bible and possible interpretations of it. In 1835–36, David Strauss wrote a book called *Das Leben Jesu kritisch bearbeitet*, which attempted to apply historical and literary criteria to the Holy Book and the Jesus figure by removing the aura of mysticism which had traditionally enveloped them. The book aroused European interest, but did not provoke one word of comment on Arnold's part.

What is probably most surprising is Arnold's complete silence in regard to the novel, which definitely asserted its raison d être during the years when Arnold was an active writer. The 19th century novel had action, wholeness and a message, i.e. three key Arnoldian demands on literature. But the novel did not attract him as a social document, which is not a little surprising considering the social conditions that are evoked by Dickens and Balzac. And Arnold did not have an eye for the potential of the narrative technique that the 19th century novels embody.

That is the more remarkable in that there is considerable resemblance between the approaches to character we find in, for example, Dickens' novels and Arnold's essays. Arnold learned of Sainte-Beuve that it was necessary to take the detailed biography of a character into consideration if you want to achieve a reliable appreciation of his work. Arnold used the same technique in some of his essays. *Mutatis mutandis*, that was also the procedure adopted by Dickens, who postulated a reliable relation between biographical background and character. The behaviour of Miss Havisham in *Great Expectations* is explained in terms of her life story.

Conclusion

"Unless I mistake it, it is precisely the interest which he had in education, politics, and religion which makes his criticism original," wrote H.W.Garrod in 1931.[1]

That statement epitomizes 20th century academia's opinion of Arnold as a critic: it is not his activity as a literary theorist that comes first to later critics' minds. To a great extent, the verdict is justifiable: Arnold was not concerned with literature *per se*, and our modern concept of a literary work as a synthesis of content of form would have seemed entirely off the point to him. That was not what he understood by 'wholeness'.

J.P. Jump suggests, very plausibly, that "the relative uniformity of literary training and experience, and consequently of reading habits" exempted him from "showing in some detail how in his opinion the text should be read and apprehended."[2] For once, Eliot removes the velvet glove: "And when we know his poetry, we are not surprised that in his criticism he tells us little or nothing about his experience of writing it, and that he is so little concerned with poetry from the maker's point of view."[3] Chambers puts it more tactfully: he does not think that Arnold "was ever at his best in attempting to expound the fundamental basis of poetic activity."[4] On the other hand nobody denies that Arnold was a vigilant and responsive reader, witness, for example, his essays on Homer.

However, being a literary critic was not a recognized profession when Arnold wrote. Ruskin, Pater, Stuart Mill and a host of "ordinary" journalists had other axes to grind. And Taine's schematic and biologically inspired theory was not one in a long series of theoretical dissertations, but one chapter in a several hundred pages long literary history. Sainte-Beuve used an author's biography to explain his work as a whole, not to analyse its details.

In the preface to *Essays in Criticism* (1865), Arnold calls himself a "transcendentalist" because he recognizes that he does not want to restrict himself to one discipline, but considers literary criticism a member of a family of metaphysical abstractions applying to, but rising above, compartmentalized political, religious, social, and human issues. Arnold's "culture" is discernible as the fruit of such thinking. His criticism is directed not only upon works of art, but also upon society and life in general.[5] As he sees it, criticism is a contribution to life's spiritual dimension, and literary criticism is part of a synthesis, an ancillary discipline that cannot and should not stand alone, but is always embedded in the Great Vision. Literature is a function of something else, serving as a confirmation, an illustration, or an explanation of something beyond itself, be it national character, social conditions, or human predicament. In *Essays in Criticism*, Arnold describes the damage that can be done to the literary and intellectual life of a nation "by the lack of any widespread belief in the validity of standards of criticism."[6]

That is why formal and other technical matters had to be pushed into the background. For his theoretical discussion of content, Arnold drew support from Aristotle's *Poetics* – Arnold's idea of 'action' is borrowed from the Greek philosopher – but the Stagyrite's detailed analysis of the formal features of a written presentation was never even hinted at by Arnold. He paid no attention to the aesthetic aspect of his writings, and he never considered his essays in terms of works of art. He never collected his observations into a *magnum opus*, and, unlike one of his mentors, Sainte-Beuve, he never aspired to, or reached, a metaphysical level with reflections on a critic's function and position.

Literature was to be a source of pleasure, but it was pleasure as Arnold saw it. The purpose of literature should be to "ennoble and sublime" the soul.[7] His concern is not about what literature "is", but what it "does", and since there are limits to what moral standards any form can inculcate, the emphasis naturally falls on content. Arnold's beloved "free play of the mind" did not include pondering on what tools a writer has at his disposal, and how he could make the best use of them.

In Arnold's opinion, writers were not supposed to "create art", but to provide insight and to promote what he considered the common good. He did not want to tickle his readers' aesthetic sense, but to make them aware of their moral responsibility.

Poetry to Arnold was to be a *magister vitae* (originally a Ciceronian idea), but the teaching evidently did not necessitate illustration or exemplification. The subject matter which criticism should most seek is "to know the best that is known or thought in the world," and once that goal is reached, "a current of true and fresh ideas will be created."[8] As will be seen, it is not only Arnold's technical terminology that is marred by vagueness. He was not a cogent thinker, and his argumentation, such as it is, is often bizarre – or simply non-existing. Too often he does not follow the matter through, but stops half-way, which leaves the reader with a big question mark and causes Arnold's criticism to seem superficial or poorly substantiated.

Thus, the short essay *How Literature Interprets*[9] comes to nothing because several pages are spent on the fact that poetry *does* interpret, but the essay says nothing about *how* poetry interprets, which was the purpose of the title. And he took Goethe's suggestion that familiarity with criticism precedes the creation of poetry at face value without trying to explicate it. Goethe argues his case, but Arnold just mentions the idea (without giving the source) and swiftly passes on to something else. And the many potentially fertile ideas that are found in Arnold's letters to Clough are repeated, but never properly elaborated in his essays.

Arnold's critical pronouncements are often value judgements disguised as axiomatic *constats*, categorical statements that are

left hanging in the air without being properly argued or expli-
cated. It is as if Arnold has reached the end of the road by the
time he has stated his favourite opinion.

Paradoxes and contradictions do occur: Arnold admires the
Classics for their thoughts, but returns again and again to the
necessity of finding "fresh ideas", although he is generally suspi-
cious of originality. Criticism is to keep clear of all "practical
matter" at the same time as it is required to "see things as they
really are." He expresses some interest in an outside authority
(not like the French Academy, though) that could lay down
standards and serve as a guide for fledgling authors. On the
other hand, he pays tribute to the individual's introspection
("looking into ourselves", "our best self") as the ultimate source
of right reason.

It is a critic's task, Arnold held, to "see things as they really
are". Yet he was apparently blind to the numerous literary
descriptions of the social unrest that was brewing right under
his nose. A crowd's peaceful trespassing into a fenced-off park
aroused his indignation. He saw it as a dangerous sign of social
disruption. The disestablishment of the Irish Church was, as
he saw it, a suspicious and subversive development because it
was divisive, which threatened Arnold's peace of mind.
Arnold's critical oeuvre dates, to a great extent, from the
decades when Marx was in England and based the theories of
Das Kapital (1848) on the actually existing appalling condi-
tions of a large segment of the contemporary English
population. Unlike Disraeli, Arnold saw no possible *literary*
material in those events. Arnold would no doubt have called
himself a socially responsible person, yet he passed it all over
in silence.

Cockshut calls Arnold "a brilliant rhetorician",[10] a state-
ment that would seem to require some qualification. Arnold
appeals to his readers, trying to ingratiate himself with them
by inviting them to use their common sense: "Surely, dear
reader you must agree that . . . " is the between-the-lines tech-
nique used in many passages. Yet Arnold's texts do not read as

oratorical masterpieces, not least because he repeats his favourite maxims *ad nauseam.* The *magister vitae* idea is the *basso ostinato* of most what he put to paper. He held an ideological and teleological view of literature, which makes his style at the same time coaxing and insistent. The 1853 *Preface* stands in a slightly awkward position when compared with Arnold's later critical output. It is the work of a young poet and critic groping for a foothold, yet dimly aware of the direction in which he wants to go. In his later essays, Arnold disengaged himself from his allegiance to drama and found a framework with which his ideas worked hand in glove.

With all the above reservations, some of which may be biased by a 21st century paradigm, it should not be forgotten that Arnold had a well-developed and sensitive literary sense, and that much of his criticism of the Romantic poets has stood the test of time, also because, in the case of the Romanticists, he endeavoured to give a balanced verdict in that he tended to be guided at least as much by his fine ear for poetry as by his moralizing Absolutes. He wanted to change the Romantic idiom, but was, by his own admission, not a systematic person who relied on his gut feeling.

He wrote essays on most of the Romantic poets. He points out that Wordsworth is better as a poet than as a philosopher. He admires not only Keats' genius, but also his stamina ("the thing to be seized is, that Keats had flint and iron in him, that he had character"), and he notes that too frequently the straining after sensuous effects relegates content ("idea") to an inferior position. Actually, Arnold's treatment of Keats is reminiscent of Eliot's treatment of Arnold. Arnold finds Shelley's philosophy shallow and flimsy; he adopts verbatim Goethe's verdict on Byron, "an excellent poet, but a mediocre thinker", and he finds that Coleridge makes things unduly complicated for his readers.

Arnold takes up a cautious and hesitant attitude to contemporary writers and movements. Most of them, he finds, do not bear closer scrutiny. He barely mentions Browning, and he

Chapelan, Maurice (ed.), *Sainte-Beuve, Pensées et Maximes.* Bernard Grasset, 1955.

Clough, Arthur Hugh, *Poems and Prose Remains, edited by his Wife*, 2 vols. London: Macmillan, 1869 .

Connell, W. F., *The Educational Thought and Influence of Matthew Arnold.* London, 1950.

Corbière-Grille, Gisèle (ed.), *Critique de Sainte-Beuve.* Paris: Nouvelles Editions Debresse, 1987.

Coulling, Sidney, *Matthew Arnold and his Critics: A Study of Arnold's Controversies.* Ohio University Press, 1974 .

Culler, A. Dwight, *Imaginative Reason: The Poetry of Matthew Arnold.* Yale University Press, 1966.

Cumberlege, Geoffrey (ed.), *Gulliver's Travels: The Tale of a Tub, Battle of the Books, etc. by Jonathan Swift.* Oxford University Press, repr. 1947.

Dawson, Carl & Pfordresker, John (eds.), *Matthew Arnold: Prose Writings.* London: Routledge & Kegan Paul, 1979.

DeLaura, David J. (ed.), *Matthew Arnold, A collection of Critical Essays.* Prentice Hall, 1973.

DeLaura, David J., 'Arnold and Literary Criticism': (i) Critical Ideas in Allott, Kenneth (ed.), *Matthew Arnold: Writers and their Background.* London, 1975.

Doyon, René-Louis & Marchèsne, Charles (eds.), *Port-Royal, édition documentaire.* Paris, 1926.

Eckermann, Johann Peter, *Gespräche mit Goethe in den letzten Jahren seines Lebens.* Brockhaus Wiesbaden, 1959.

The Edinburgh Review 1802 et seq.

Eliot, T. S., *Selected Essays.* London: Faber & Faber, 1932.

Eliot, T. S., *The Idea of a Christian Society.* London: Faber & Faber, 1939.

Eliot, T. S., *The Use of Poetry and the Use of Criticism.* London: Faber & Faber, 1970.

Fairley, Barker, *Goethe as Revealed in his Poetry.* Chicago, 1932.

Fayrolle, Roger, *Sainte-Beuve et le XVIIIᵉ siècle, ou comment les révolutions arrivent.* Paris: Armand Colin, 1972.

Fells, John S., *The Touchstone of Matthew Arnold.* New Haven, Connecticut, n.d.

Ford, Boris (ed.), *The Pelican Guide to English Literature, vol. 6: From Dickens to Hardy.* Penguin Books, 1958.

Furrer, Paul, *Der Einfluss Sainte-Beuve auf die Kritik Matthew Arnolds.* Zurich, 1920.

Garrod, H. W., *Poetry and the Criticism of Life.* Oxford, 1931.

Giraud, Victor (ed.), *Sainte-Beuve, Charles-Augustin, Nouveaux Lundis I–XIII, 1864–70.* Paris, 1903.

Goode, John & Hardy, Barbara (eds.), *Major Victorian Poets: Reconsiderations.* London: Routlege & Kegan Paul, 1969.

Gottfried, Leon, *Matthew Arnold and the Romantics.* University of Nebraska Press, 1963.

Guérin, Maurice de, *Oeuvres completes*, 2 vols. Société les Belles Lettres. Paris, 1947.

Haenelt, Karin, *Studien zu Goethes Literarischer Kritik. Ihre Voraussetzungen und Möglichkeiten.* Frankfurt am Main: Peter Lang, 1985.

Hatfield, Henry, *Goethe: A Critical Introduction.* Harvard University Press, 1964.

Helsinger, Elizabeth K., *Ruskin and the Art of the Beholder.* Harvard University Press, 1982.

Holloway, John, *The Victorian Sage: Studies in Argument.* London: Macmillan, 1953.

Honan, Park, *Matthew Arnold. A Life.* Harvard University Press, 1983.

Houghton, Walter E., *The Victorian Frame of Mind.* Yale University Press, 1957.

James, D. G., *Matthew Arnold and the Decline of English Romanticism.* Oxford, 1961.

Johnson, E. D. H., *The Alien Vision of Victorian Poetry: Sources of the Poetic Imagination Tennyson, Browning, and Arnold.* Princeton University Press, 1952.

Johnson, Samuel, *The Lives of the English Poets.* London, 1779–81.

Johnson, W. Stacey, *The Voices of Matthew Arnold: An Essay in Criticism.* New Haven, 1961.

Jump, J. D., 'Matthew Arnold' in Boris Ford (ed.), *The Pelican Guide to English Literature,* vol. 6. Penguin Books, 1958.

Kolb, Jack (ed.), *The Letters of Arthur Henry Hallam.* Ohio State University Press, 1981.

Lamb, Charles, *Essays of Elia 1820–33.* Oxford University Press, repr. 1946.

Leavis, F. R., '*Arnold as Critic.*' *Scrutiny VII*, 1938.

Legouis, Emile & Cazamian, Louis, *A History of English Literature.* Revised edition, London: Dent & Sons, 1945.

Leroy, Maxime, *La Pensée de Sainte-Beuve.* Gallimard, 1940.

Levine, George & Madden, William A., (ed.), *The Art of Victorian Prose.* Oxford University Press, 1968.

Lowry, H. F., *Matthew Arnold and the Modern Spirit.* Princeton University Press, 1941.

Lowry, Howard Foster, (ed.), *The Letters of Matthew Arnold to Arthur Hugh Clough.* Oxford University Press, 1932, repr. 1968.

Lowry, Howard Foster, Young, Karl & Dunn, Waldo Hilary (eds.), *The Note-Books of Matthew Arnold.* Oxford University Press, 1952.

McCarthy, Patrick J., *Matthew Arnold and the Three Classes.* Columbia University Press, 1964.

Machann, Clinton, *Matthew Arnold: A Literary Life.* Macmillan, 1998.

Madden, William A., *Matthew Arnold: A Study of the Aesthetic Temperament in Victorian England.* Bloomington, Indiana, 1967.

Mill, John Stuart, *Dissertations and Discussions.* London, 1859.

Mill, John Stuart, *Letters* (ed. H. S. R. Eliot). London, 1910.

Morpurgo, J. E. (ed.), *Charles Lamb and Elia.* Penguin Books, 1948.

Moxon, T. A. (ed.), *Aristotle's Poetics, Demetrius on Style and Other Classical Writings on Criticism.* Everyman's Library 901. London: Dent, 1943.

Neff, Emery, *Carlyle.* New York, 1932.

Neimann, Fraser, *Essays, Letters and Reviews by Matthew Arnold.* London, 1960.

Newman, F. W. *Phases of Faith.* London: Trübner, 1881.

Newman, J. H., *Essays on the Development of Christian Doctrine.* London: Longmans Green, 1891.

Nietzsche, Friedrich, *Unzeitgemässe Betrachtungen,* 1873–76.

Nietzsche, Friedrich, *Schopenhauer als Erzieher,* 1874.

Olsen, Flemming, *Thomas Arnold the Teacher.* Danish University of Education Press, 2004.

Olsen, Flemming, *Between Positivism and T. S. Eliot: Imagism and T. E. Hulme.* University Press of Southern Denmark, 2008.

Olsen, Flemming, *Leigh Hunt and 'What Is Poetry?' Romanticism and the Purpose of Poetry*. Sussex Academic Press, 2011.

Olsen, Flemming, *Eliot's Objective Correlative: Tradition or Individual Talent?* Sussex Academic Press, 2012.

Paul, H. W., *Matthew Arnold*. London: Macmilllan, 1920.

The Quarterly Review 1809 et seq.

Renan, Ernest, *Essais de morale et de critique*. Paris: Lévy Frères, 1859.

Renan, Ernest, *Dialogues et fragments philosophiques*. Paris, 1876.

Riede, David G., *Matthew Arnold and the Betrayal of Language*. University Press of Virginia, 1988.

Robbins, William, *The Ethical Idealism of Matthew Arnold: A Study of the Nature and Sources of his Moral and Religious Ideas*. London: Heinemann, 1959.

Roe, F. W., *Thomas Carlyle as a Critic of Art*. London, 1910.

Roper, Alan, *Arnold's Poetic Landscapes*. Johns Hopkins Press, 1969.

Ruskin, John, *Modern Painters, vol. III*. London, 1856.

Russell, George W. E. (ed.), *Letters of Matthew Arnold 1848–88*. 2 vols. New York & London: Macmillan, 1895.

Sainte-Beuve, Charles Augustin, *Portraits littéraires I–III*. Paris 1862–64.

Sainte-Beuve, Charles Augustin, *Portraits contemporains I–IV, 1869–71*. Paris, 1871.

Sainte-Beuve, Charles Augustin, *Premiers Lundis I–III*. Paris, 1874–75.

Saintsbury, George E. B., *A History of Nineteenth-Century Literature*. London, 1916.

Schopenhauer, Arthur, *Die Welt als Wille und Vorstellung*, 1818.

Seigel, Jules Paul, *Thomas Carlyle: The Critical Heritage*. London: Routledge & Kegan Paul, 1971.

Sherman, S. P., *Matthew Arnold*. New York: Peter Smith, 1932.

Stange, G. Robert, *Matthew Arnold: The Poet as Humanist*. Princeton University Press, 1967.

Steinmetz, Martha S., *Die ideen geschichtliche Bedeutung Matthew Arnolds*. Tübingen, 1932.

Stephen, Leslie, *Studies of a Biographer*. Vol. II, London, 1898.

Strachey, Lytton, *Eminent Victorians*. London, 1918.

Strauss, David. F., *The Life of Jesus* (trans. G. Eliot). London: Swan Sonnenschein, 1892.

Super, R. H., (ed.), *The Complete Prose Works of Matthew Arnold.* 11 vols., Ann Arbor: University of Michigan Press, 1960–77.

Super, R. H., (ed.), *Matthew Arnold, Culture and Anarchy. (The Complete Prose Works of Matthew Arnold, vol. V).* University of Michigan Press, 1965.

Super, R. H., *The Time-Spirit of Matthew Arnold.* Ann Arbor, 1970.

Super, R. H. (ed), *Matthew Arnold: Lectures and Essays in Criticism.* University of Michigan Press, 1973.

Super, R. H., 'Arnold and Literary Criticism : (ii) Critical Practice' in Allott, Kenneth (ed.), *Matthew Arnold: Writers and their Background.* London, 1975.

Swift, Jonathan, *A Full and True Account of the Battle Fought Last Friday between the Ancient and the Modern Books* in *Gulliver's Travels, The Tale of a Tub, etc.* Oxford Editions of Standard Authors. Oxford University Press, 1947.

Thorpe, Michael (ed.), *Clough: The Critical Heritage.* London: Routledge & Kegan Paul, 1972.

Tinker, C. B. & Lowry, H.F. (eds.), *The Poetry of Matthew Arnold. A Commentary.* Oxford University Press, 1940.

Tinker, C. B. & Lowry, H. F. (eds.), *The Poetical Works of Matthew Arnold.* New Complete Edition. Oxford Editions of Standard Authors. Oxford University Press, 1950.

Trilling, Lionel, *Matthew Arnold.* Revised edition, New York, 1949.

Varenne, Gaston, *Goethe devant la Nature et l'Art.* Paris: Editions Bernard Grasset, 1943.

Viëtor, Karl, *Goethe, the Thinker.* Trans. B. Q. Morgan. Cambridge, Mass. 1950.

Waddington, Samuel, *Arthur Hugh Clough.* London, 1883.

Warren, Alba H. Jr., *English Poetic Theory, 1825–1865.* Princeton Studies in English, No. 29. Reprint – Frank Cass & Co. Ltd., 1966.

Whitridge, Arnold (ed.), *Unpublished Letters of Matthew Arnold.* Yale University Press, 1923.

Willey, Basil, *Nineteenth Century Studies: Coleridge to Matthew Arnold.* London, 1950.

Wilson, J. Dover (ed.), *Culture and Anarchy.* Cambridge University Press, 1955.

INDEX